Palgrave Studies in US Elections

Series Editor
Luke Perry
Utica College
Utica, NY, USA

This Pivot series, established in collaboration with the Utica College Center of Public Affairs and Election Research, brings together cutting-edge work in US Politics focused on trends and issues surrounding local, state, and federal elections. Books in this series may cover but are not limited to topics such as voting behavior, campaign management, policy considerations, electoral social movements, and analysis of significant races. While welcoming all projects on US elections within and across all three levels of government, this series proceeds from the truism that all politics is fundamentally local. As such, we are especially interested in research on state and local elections such as mayoral races, gubernatorial races, and congressional elections, with particular focus on how state/local electoral trends influence national electoral politics, and vice versa. This series is open to any relevant scholar and all methodological approaches.

More information about this series at
http://www.palgrave.com/gp/series/16164

Luke Perry

Donald Trump and the 2018 Midterm Battle for Central New York

palgrave
macmillan

Luke Perry
Utica College
Utica, NY, USA

Palgrave Studies in US Elections
ISBN 978-3-030-13022-0   ISBN 978-3-030-13023-7 (eBook)
https://doi.org/10.1007/978-3-030-13023-7

Library of Congress Control Number: 2019933172

© The Editor(s) (if applicable) and The Author(s) 2019
This work is subject to copyright. All rights are solely and exclusively licensed by the Publisher, whether the whole or part of the material is concerned, specifically the rights of translation, reprinting, reuse of illustrations, recitation, broadcasting, reproduction on microfilms or in any other physical way, and transmission or information storage and retrieval, electronic adaptation, computer software, or by similar or dissimilar methodology now known or hereafter developed.
The use of general descriptive names, registered names, trademarks, service marks, etc. in this publication does not imply, even in the absence of a specific statement, that such names are exempt from the relevant protective laws and regulations and therefore free for general use.
The publisher, the authors and the editors are safe to assume that the advice and information in this book are believed to be true and accurate at the date of publication. Neither the publisher nor the authors or the editors give a warranty, express or implied, with respect to the material contained herein or for any errors or omissions that may have been made. The publisher remains neutral with regard to jurisdictional claims in published maps and institutional affiliations.

Cover illustration © Bitboxx.com

This Palgrave Pivot imprint is published by the registered company Springer Nature Switzerland AG.
The registered company address is: Gewerbestrasse 11, 6330 Cham, Switzerland

For countless journalists at local media outlets who diligently cover electoral campaigns for the benefit of our democracy. And my daughter who wants to be president and a librarian.

Contents

1. Introduction to the 2018 Midterm, NY-19, NY-22, and NY-24   1
2. Issues and Messaging   25
3. Polling   69
4. Who Won and Why   91

LIST OF FIGURES

Fig. 1.1	NY-19 before 2010 redistricting. (Source: http://www.latfor.state.ny.us/maps/2002cong/fc019.pdf)	7
Fig. 1.2	NY-19 after 2010 redistricting	8
Fig. 1.3	NY-22 before 2010 redistricting. (Source: http://www.latfor.state.ny.us/maps/2002cong/fc022.pdf)	9
Fig. 1.4	NY-22 after 2010 redistricting. (Source: http://www.latfor.state.ny.us/maps/2012c/CD_map_rep_22.pdf)	10
Fig. 1.5	NY-24 before 2010 redistricting. (Source: http://www.latfor.state.ny.us/maps/2002cong/fc024.pdf)	11
Fig. 1.6	NY-24 after 2010 redistricting. (Source: http://www.latfor.state.ny.us/maps/2012c/CD_map_rep_24.pdf)	12
Fig. 4.1	Real GDP: percent change from preceding quarter	109

List of Tables

Table 1.1	Voter registration in NY-24 post-redistricting	13
Table 1.2	Voter registration in NY-22 post-redistricting	13
Table 1.3	Voter registration in NY-19 post-redistricting	14
Table 1.4	Recent NY-19 representatives	14
Table 1.5	Recent NY-22 representatives	15
Table 1.6	Recent NY-24 representatives	15
Table 1.7	County-level results for presidential elections in NY-19	16
Table 1.8	Registered partisans in NY-19 (November 1, 2016)	16
Table 1.9	2016 Election results in NY-19	17
Table 1.10	County-level results for presidential elections in NY-22	19
Table 1.11	Registered partisans in NY-22 (November 1, 2016)	19
Table 1.12	2016 Election results in NY-22	20
Table 1.13	County-level results for presidential elections in NY-24	21
Table 1.14	Registered partisans in NY-24 (November 1, 2016)	21
Table 1.15	2016 election results in NY-24	21
Table 3.1	August NY-19 poll: candidate support	70
Table 3.2	August NY-19 poll: gender and geography	70
Table 3.3	August NY-19 poll: favorability of candidates	71
Table 3.4	August NY-19 poll: presidential approval rating	71
Table 3.5	August NY-19 poll: party control of house	72
Table 3.6	Monmouth NY-19 poll: candidate support	73
Table 3.7	Monmouth NY-19 poll: interest in house election	73
Table 3.8	Monmouth NY-19 poll: President Trump's approval rating	73
Table 3.9	Monmouth NY-19 poll: party control of house	73
Table 3.10	Monmouth NY-19 poll: important issues	74
Table 3.11	Siena NY-19 poll: candidate support	75
Table 3.12	Siena NY-19 poll: gender and geography	75

Table 3.13	Siena NY-19 poll: favorability of candidates	75
Table 3.14	Siena NY-19 poll: presidential approval rating	76
Table 3.15	Siena NY-19 poll: party control of house	76
Table 3.16	Zogby analytics poll	77
Table 3.17	Siena NY-22 poll: candidate support	79
Table 3.18	Siena NY-22 poll: favorability of candidates	79
Table 3.19	Siena NY-22 poll: gender and geography	79
Table 3.20	Siena NY-22 poll: party control of house	80
Table 3.21	Siena NY-22 poll: presidential approval rating	80
Table 3.22	Siena NY-22 poll: candidate support	81
Table 3.23	Siena NY-22 poll: favorability of candidates	81
Table 3.24	Siena NY-22 poll: gender and geography	81
Table 3.25	Siena NY-22 poll: party control of house	82
Table 3.26	Siena NY-22 poll: presidential approval rating	82
Table 3.27	Siena NY-24 poll: candidate support	83
Table 3.28	Siena NY-24 poll: geography and gender	84
Table 3.29	Siena NY-24 poll: favorability of candidates	84
Table 3.30	Siena NY-24 poll: party control of house	84
Table 3.31	Siena NY-24 poll: presidential approval rating	85
Table 3.32	Siena NY-24 poll: candidate support	86
Table 3.33	Siena NY-24 poll: geography and gender	86
Table 3.34	Siena NY-24 poll: favorability of candidates	86
Table 3.35	Siena NY-24 poll: presidential approval rating	87
Table 3.36	Siena NY-24 poll: party control of house	87
Table 4.1	NY-19 election night totals	94
Table 4.2	NY-19 election day results by county	95
Table 4.3	NY-19 election day margin of victory by county	95
Table 4.4	NY-19 election day voter turnout	96
Table 4.5	Comparing 2016 and 2018 NY-19 results	96
Table 4.6	NY-22 election night totals	97
Table 4.7	NY-22 election day results by county	97
Table 4.8	NY-22 election day margin of victory by county	98
Table 4.9	2018 NY-22 election day voter turnout	99
Table 4.10	Comparing 2016 and 2018 results in NY-22	100
Table 4.11	2018 NY-24 election day results	100
Table 4.12	NY-24 election day results by county	100
Table 4.13	2018 NY-24 election day margin of victory by county	101
Table 4.14	Comparing 2016 and 2018 results in NY-24	101
Table 4.15	2018 NY-24 election day voter turnout	101
Table 4.16	Presidential approval rating and midterm gains/losses	102

CHAPTER 1

Introduction to the 2018 Midterm, NY-19, NY-22, and NY-24

Abstract This chapter introduces the book and the three districts examined in relation to the 2018 election: NY-19, NY-22, and NY-24.

Keywords John Faso • Claudia Tenney • John Katko • Antonio Delgado • Anthony Brindisi • Dana Balter • 2018 Midterm election • Donald Trump • upstate New York • NY-19 • NY-22 • NY-24

The 2018 election was the first after a heavily contested 2016 campaign that witnessed the surprise election of a political novice to the White House. After two years in office, Donald Trump, conservative hero to his fervent supporters and gangster fascist to his fiercest critics, became an even more polarizing and dominant presence in U.S. politics than recent presidents. Trump was the central figure in the 2018 campaign where Democrats had not been as enthusiastic in a midterm election since 2006.

This book examines three neighboring and competitive House races in Central New York, districts 19, 22, and 24, which analysts believed were an important component to Democratic efforts to retake the House. Each district was home to a Republican incumbent seeking to navigate the Trump presidency. The respective campaigns reflected the division and dysfunction that has come to define U.S. politics, including fundamentally different perceptions of healthcare, taxes, and immigration, to animosity

© The Author(s) 2019
L. Perry, *Donald Trump and the 2018 Midterm Battle for Central New York*, Palgrave Studies in US Elections,
https://doi.org/10.1007/978-3-030-13023-7_1

surrounding race and the resistance, to "fake news" and the personal style of politics Trump has popularized.

In the end, the outcome of these races exhibited how closely aligning with President Trump was more hurtful than helpful for Republicans. Trump was a boon for Democratic candidates, even ones who hardly mentioned him. More subtly, Trump's efforts to remake the Republican Party in his image have not been uniformly embraced in more moderately conservative parts of the country, such as Upstate New York.

National Climate

Open seats are typically closely contested. There were over 50 open seats in 2018, a record amount.[1] There was also little doubt that most incumbents would be reelected, per historical norms. This was the case for nearly 90 percent of House incumbents in 2018, which is slightly lower than historical norms, while illustrating the enduring strength of incumbency advantage. Incumbents typically enjoy several electoral benefits, including increased name recognition, fundraising advantages, franking privileges, and greater ability to deter quality challengers from running.[2] Though certainly advantageous, incumbency does not guarantee electoral success.

House Republicans faced a highly unfavorable national climate in 2018. The president's party has lost an average of 25 House seats during midterm elections since 1946. The party of presidents polling under 50 percent, as President Trump did consistently during his first two years in office, loses an average of 37 seats.[3] Only twice has the president's party gained seats. Both were exceptional situations. In 1998, Bill Clinton was impeached by House Republicans, and in 2002 George W. Bush led the immediate response to the 9/11 attacks. Both had approval ratings over 60 percent, and gains were modest, five and six seats, respectively. There was no doubt that some House GOP incumbents would be vulnerable in 2018. The question was who, and where this vulnerability would emerge.

Swing Districts

Swing districts are pivotal in competitive Congressional election cycles similar to how swing states are pivotal to presidential elections.[4] They receive limited scholarly attention because of the power of incumbency advantage and the fact that most House races are uncompetitive, an average of 70 percent of House races by some estimates, prompting signficant focus on gerrymandering.[5] Analysis of swing districts generally focuses on the rare occurrence where control of seats regularly changes between Republicans and Democrats in recent Congressional elections and/or when a district's presidential vote swings back and forth between Republican and Democratic candidates in recent presidential elections. More in-depth factors utilized to identify competitive House districts include:

1. incumbent's previous margin of victory;
2. generic Congressional ballot;
3. fundraising for incumbent compared to challenger;
4. district voting patterns in presidential elections and state legislative elections;
5. Congressional approval ratings;
6. presence or absence of scandal related to incumbent;
7. voting record; and
8. political experience of challenger.[6]

Competitiveness can also be broken down to county-level analysis. One relevant consideration was presidential "pivot counties," counties that voted for Barack Obama in 2008 and 2012 and Donald Trump in 2016.[7] Aggregating this precise geographic measurement helps illustrate larger trends around the country regarding the location of partisan swings. Most pivot counties were located in the Midwest and Northeast. For instance, Iowa (31), Wisconsin (23), Minnesota (19), and New York (18) were home to the most pivot counties.

There is a large range with the number of counties per state. Delaware has 3 counties, while Texas has 254. Another way to analyze this data is by the percentage of counties within a state that are pivot counties. The Midwest and Northeast were similarly prevalent among states with the highest percentage of pivot counties: Maine (50 percent), Delaware (33 percent), Wisconsin (32 percent), Iowa (31 percent), New Hampshire (30 percent), and New York (29 percent).[8] New York was clearly home to a nationally significant amount of pivot counties in 2018. These were nearly uniformly located upstate. Suffolk County was the only one of 18 pivot counties in New York to be located within New York City.

Upstate New York Politics

"Upstate New York" can be a broad and all-encompassing term, particularly to non-New Yorkers. This typically refers to all of New York State north of New York City and its immediate suburbs in Rockland County and Westchester County. Within upstate are several distinct regions, such as the North Country, Capital District, Central New York, the Southern Tier, the Finger Lakes, Hudson Valley, and Western New York.

A sizable cluster of pivot counties are found in the middle of New York State, encompassing several of these regions and various counties, including Sullivan County, Otsego County, Broome County, Madison County, Cortland County, Cayuga County, and Oswego County. These seven counties span three Congressional districts: NY-19, NY-22, and NY-24. All three of these districts have also swung this century between Democratic and Republican House representatives, making them a prime target for Congressional Campaign Committees.[9] This was particularly the case for Democrats, who have unsuccessfully targeted these seats in recent election cycles. As a result, Central New York, and NY-19, NY-22, and NY-24, in particular, have been an interesting and important focus in the realm of swing districts and competitive House elections.

The fact that Republicans have held all three of these seats since 2014, when John Katko was elected in NY-24, and even longer in NY-22 and NY-19, may come as a surprise to those unfamiliar with the nuances of New York State politics. New York State has voted Democratic in presidential elections every cycle since 1988. Every U.S. Senator from New York this century has been a Democrat and each governor since 2006 has been a Democrat. At the same time, an "upstate/downstate divide" is common parlance in New York State politics. Over 9 million New Yorkers reside in 468 square miles of New York City, the most populated city in the country, exceeding the population of 40 of the country's 50 states.[10] New York City residents, coupled with suburban residents in Westchester County and Rockland County, account for the majority of the state's population. Upstate New Yorkers reside in the remaining 55,000 square miles of the state.

Upstate New Yorkers commonly feel marginalized and underrepresented in state government generally, and positions of leadership, in particular. These feelings are exacerbated by subcultural variance, most prominently, the contrast of rural norms with urban/suburban norms, and demographic factors, including identity and class differences. In many ways, Upstate New York is as comparable to Midwestern culture as the Northeast.

Partisan politics is also a powerful consideration. Upstate is predominately Republican, except for rustbelt cities, such as Utica and Syracuse, while downstate is extraordinarily Democratic. As a result, there are ongoing political tensions between upstate Republicans, who equate Democratic control of state governance with the representation of downstate interests, and prominent Downstate Democrats, such as Governor Andrew Cuomo. For instance, Governor Cuomo professed his love for Upstate New York following the 2018 election. "I'm upstate's voice," Cuomo stated in addressing concerns about adequately representing upstate interests, "They have a very loud voice in the (negotiating) room. It's my voice."[11] This sentiment is not shared by many upstate, Republicans or Democrats, where the governor is much less popular than downstate.

Upstate Republicans tend to be fiscally conservative and socially more liberal than their national counterparts. For instance, tax cuts and deregulation are generally well received, while there is less resistance to more progressive approaches to social issues, such as LGBTQ rights, criminal justice reform, and healthcare, than the GOP at large. One consideration is how New York is more secular than the Southeast, the geographic base of the Republican Party. Another consideration is the value placed on independence and bipartisanship upstate. Citizens generally embrace the notion that upstate representatives of both parties need to work together to address lasting systematic problems stemming from postindustrialism, including economic underdevelopment, population loss, a shrinking tax base, deteriorating infrastructure, and medically underserved communities, to name a few.

The ascendance of New Yorkers to prominent positions of national political power makes this backdrop of state politics all the more interesting. The 2016 presidential elections pitted two nominees from New York against one another. The outcome not only elevated a New Yorker to the White House for the first time since Franklin Roosevelt, but included Chuck Schumer becoming Senate Minority Leader. Two years later, New York's Governor and senior Senator had become two major antagonists of the president.

Key Questions

The more moderate nature of upstate Republicanism was tested in 2018 by the combination of a rightward moving GOP and an unpredictable president prioritizing personal loyalty in remaking the party in his image. Conversely, the Democrats, long disillusioned by gerrymandering, rightly viewed this election as their best chance in years to retake the House. The Iraq War was a core element of the 2006 Democratic House victory and, more specifically, crucial "partisan swing in Republican districts."[12] Would the Trump presidency and/or Republican efforts to repeal the Affordable Care Act similarly engender a Democratic victory? The short answer was "yes."

Four House incumbents in New York were defeated. For starters, Joseph Crowley (NY-14) lost to primary challenger Alexandria Ocasio-Cortez in one of the greatest upsets in modern history. Crowley was a senior and rising Democratic House leader. Ocasio-Cortez was the youngest Congresswoman ever elected and she immediately became a national sensation. The NY-11, NY-19, and NY-22 races were long and bruising campaigns that led to defeats of the only House Republican in New York City, and two freshmen Republicans in Central New York, John Faso and Claudia Tenney.

This book documents and examines in detail what happened in NY-19, NY-22, and NY-24. How did these vulnerable Republican incumbents navigate the Trump presidency? What explained their respective electoral successes and failures? What can future election analysts, journalists, organizers, and campaign operatives learn from comparative analysis of these three cases?

This book is organized into four chapters. The rest of this chapter examines each of the three districts in detail, including redistricting, partisanship, and electoral history. Chapter 2 examines prominent issues and messaging in the 2018 campaigns for NY-19, NY-22, and NY-24. Chapter 3 examines relevant polling throughout the campaign cycle. Chapter 4 explains who won and why.

The Districts

Reapportionment after the 2010 census led to redistricting in NY-19, NY-22, and NY-24 as the total number of U.S. House seats in New York was reduced to 27 from 29. NY-19 geographically expanded northward

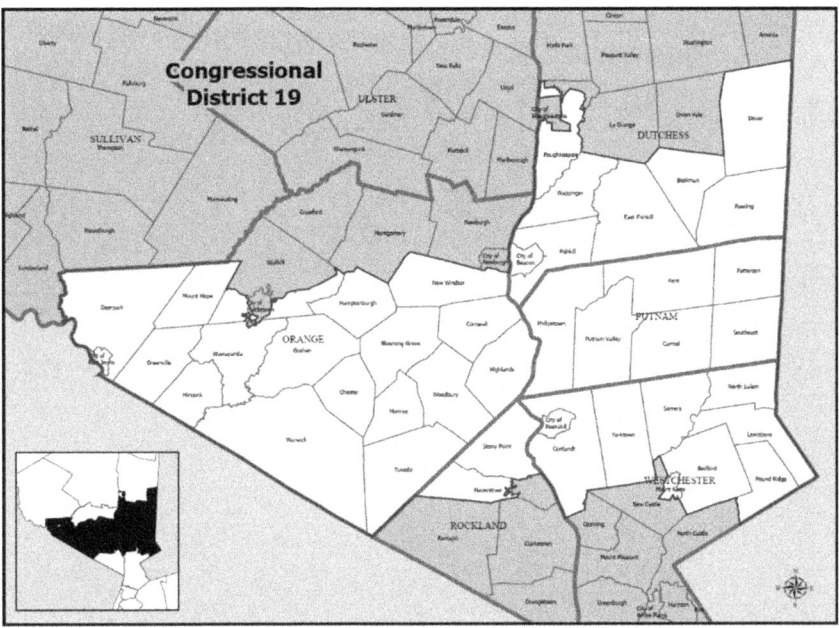

Fig. 1.1 NY-19 before 2010 redistricting. (Source: http://www.latfor.state.ny.us/maps/2002cong/fc019.pdf)

into Central New York after previously being confined to Northern suburbs of New York City. NY-22 expanded northward from Binghamton to Rome. NY-24, which comprised much of present-day NY-22, shrunk geographically as Syracuse became its metro center (Figs. 1.1, 1.2, 1.3, 1.4, 1.5, and 1.6).

Democrats have outnumbered Republicans in NY-24 since redistricting. The Democratic advantage nearly tripled between 2012 and 2018 from 5240 to 14,325. Conversely, Republicans steadily outnumbered Democrats in NY-22 by a considerable margin, 26,000–30,000. In New York, candidates can run on multiple ballot lines and often do. Conservative small party lines typically outnumber liberal small party lines in Central New York. This means that registered voters in NY-22 and NY-24 were a bit more conservative than the Democratic/Republican split conveys.

Fig. 1.2 NY-19 after 2010 redistricting

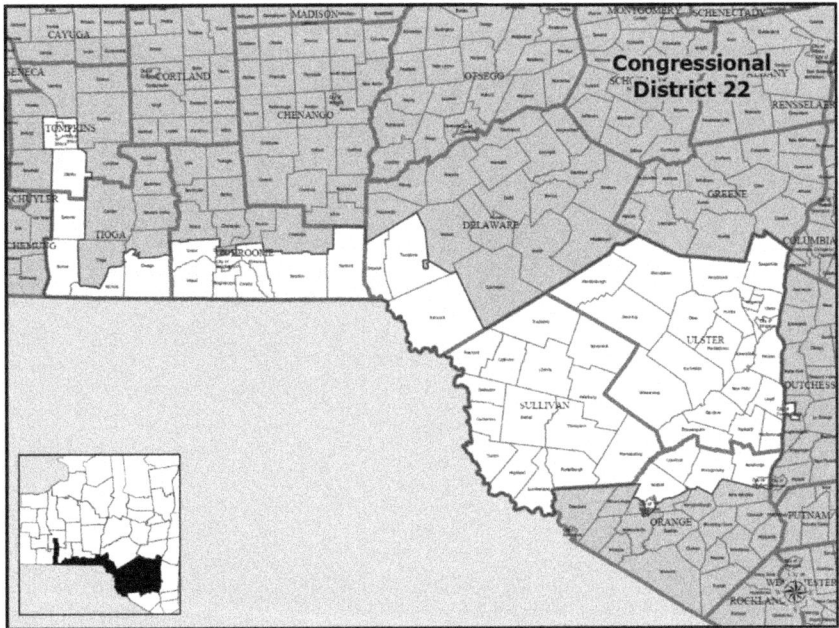

Fig. 1.3 NY-22 before 2010 redistricting. (Source: http://www.latfor.state.ny.us/maps/2002cong/fc022.pdf)

Claudia Tenney sought to publicly position herself within shifting district boundaries. Shortly after taking office Tenney said her district was "very different than the old 24th, which was a moderate district. This district (NY-22) is much more Republican than the district that Sherry Boehlert or Mike Arcuri or Richard Hanna held in the first term. I'm a perfect fit for this district for this reason."[13] The district in 2016 was slightly more Republican than NY-24 when Richard Hanna (R) was elected in 2010 (R +22,095), but much less Republican than when Michael Arcuri (D) was elected in 2006 (Republican +38,205). Data is not available for when Sherry Boehlert was elected.

NY-19 is the only district of the three to experience a flip in registered voter advantage. Republicans held a narrow registered voter advantage in NY-19 (around 3000) between 2012 and 2016, when the number of Democrats began to exceed the number of Republicans. Democrats

Fig. 1.4 NY-22 after 2010 redistricting. (Source: http://www.latfor.state.ny.us/maps/2012c/CD_map_rep_22.pdf)

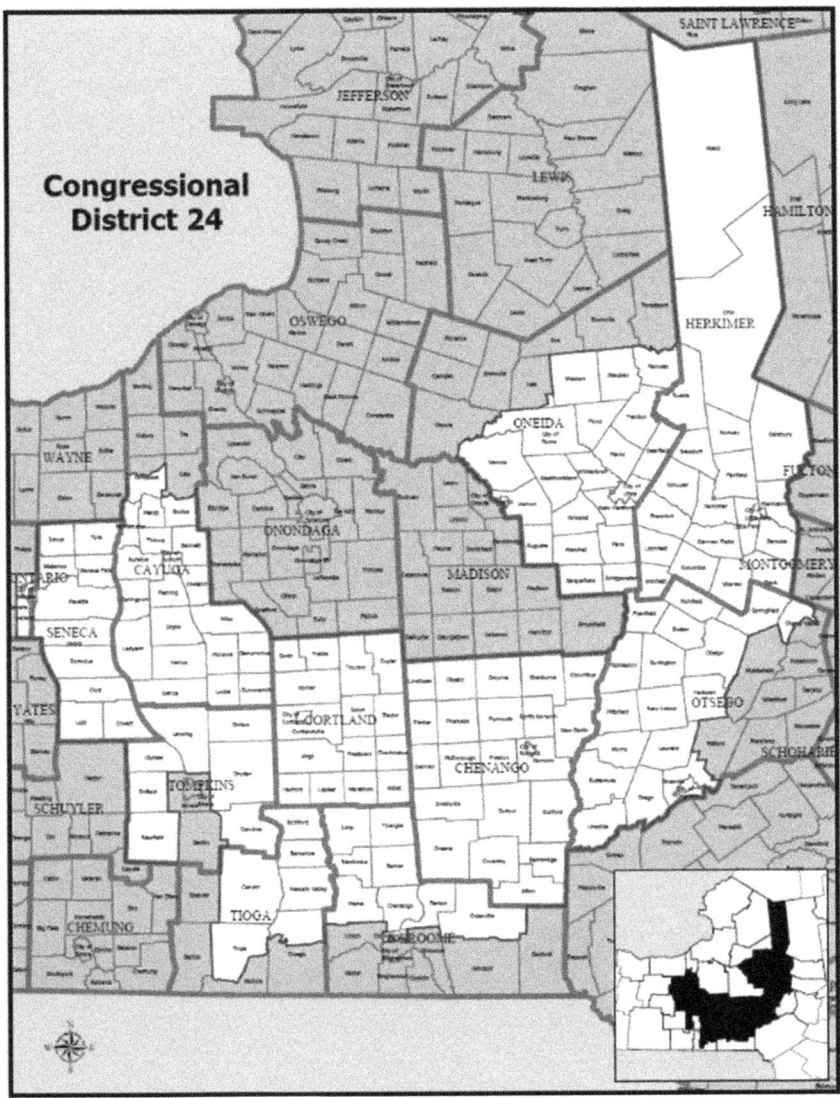

Fig. 1.5 NY-24 before 2010 redistricting. (Source: http://www.latfor.state.ny.us/maps/2002cong/fc024.pdf)

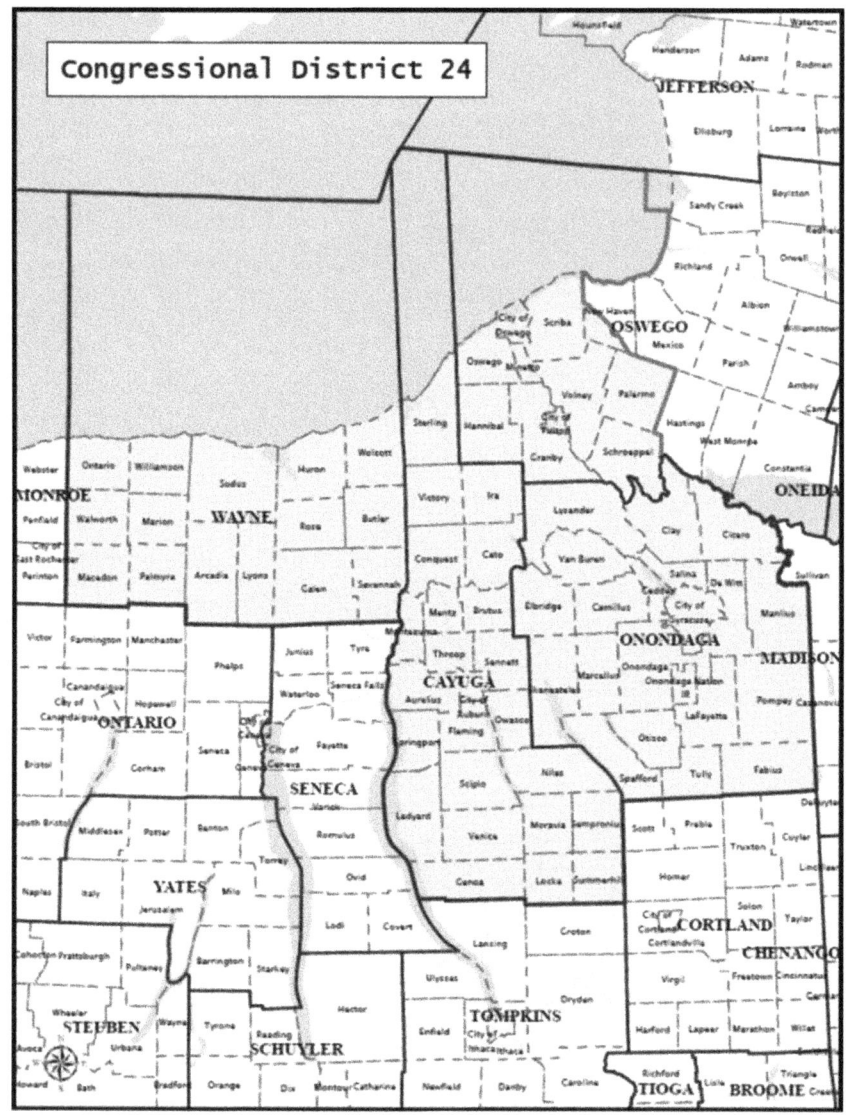

Fig. 1.6 NY-24 after 2010 redistricting. (Source: http://www.latfor.state.ny.us/maps/2012c/CD_map_rep_24.pdf)

Table 1.1 Voter registration in NY-24 post-redistricting

	Democrats	Republicans	Difference
November 2018	163,448	149,123	D +14,325
November 2017	158,857	148,540	D +10,317
November 2016	161,014	149,813	D +11,201
November 2015	153,039	145,530	D +7509
November 2014	157,184	149,704	D +7480
November 2013	156,213	150,526	D +5687
November 2012	160,716	155,476	D +5240

Source: *The New York Board of Elections*, http://www.elections.ny.gov/EnrollmentAD.html

Table 1.2 Voter registration in NY-22 post-redistricting

	Republicans	Democrats	Difference
November 2018	169,765	142,841	R +26,924
November 2017	168,715	139,832	R +28,883
November 2016	172,553	146,503	R +26,050
November 2015	165,413	137,081	R +28,332
November 2014	169,255	140,707	R +28,548
November 2013	170,207	140,842	R +29,365
November 2012	175,986	146,862	R +29,124

Source: *The New York Board of Elections*, http://www.elections.ny.gov/EnrollmentAD.html

gained over a 4000-person advantage in 2016, which held in 2017, and more than doubled in 2018 to over 11,000. This was a remarkable shift that benefitted Antonio Delgado's Democratic challenge to John Faso (Tables 1.1, 1.2, and 1.3).

Republicans have dominated control of NY-19, NY-22, and NY-24 since the 2010 redistricting, holding all three seats, every cycle but one.[14] Democrat Dan Maffei won NY-24 by 5 points in 2012 before losing to John Katko in 2014. NY-19 Republicans won by an average of 14 points between 2012 and 2016, but this was skewed by Chris Gibson's landslide reelection in 2014, as the other two margins of victory were 6 and 9 points, respectively. Similarly, NY-22 Republicans won by an average of 13 points between 2012 and 2016, but this was inflated by Richard Hanna's

Table 1.3 Voter registration in NY-19 post-redistricting

	Republicans	Democrats	Difference
November 2018	148,899	160,621	D +11,722
November 2017	147,192	151,879	D +4867
November 2016	148,635	153,104	D +4469
November 2015	143,196	142,581	R +615
November 2014	146,532	143,779	R +2753
November 2013	147,929	144,294	R +3635
November 2012	152,913	149,947	R +2966

Source: *The New York Board of Elections*, http://www.elections.ny.gov/EnrollmentAD.html

Table 1.4 Recent NY-19 representatives

	Representative	Party	Margin of victory
2016	John Faso	Republican	8.2 points
2014	Chris Gibson	Republican	28.1 points
2012	Chris Gibson	Republican	5.3 points
2010	Nan Heyworth	Republican	5.2 points
2008	John Hall	Democrat	13.1 points
2006	John Hall	Democrat	10.6 points
2004	Sue Kelly	Republican	22.8 points
2002	Sue Kelly	Republican	33.7 points
2000	Sue Kelly	Republican	20.6 points

Source: "New York's 19th Congressional District Election," *Ballotpedia*, https://ballotpedia.org/New_York%27s_19th_Congressional_District_election,_2018

20-point victory in 2012, and he ran unopposed two years later. John Katko won in 2014 and 2016, by 19 and 21 points, respectively.

By this measure alone, it may seem that none of the three districts examined here would appear ripe for a Democratic victory. Barack Obama was president; however, throughout this six-year period and two of the three election cycles were midterms. As previously noted, the president's party faces inherent challenges during midterm elections, particularly when the president is unpopular. President Obama's approval rating in November of 2014, 43 percent, mirrored that of President Trump in November of 2018.[15] The Democrats lost 63 House seats and 6 Senate seats in 2010 and 13 House seats and 9 Senate seats in 2014, enabling Republican control of Congress until 2018, the first midterm this decade under a Republican president (Tables 1.4, 1.5, and 1.6).

Table 1.5 Recent NY-22 representatives

	Representative	Party	Margivn of victory
2016	Claudia Tenney	Republican	5.4 points
2014	Richard Hanna	Republican	Unopposed
2012	Richard Hanna	Republican	20 points
2010	Maurice Hinchey	Democrat	5.1 points
2008	Maurice Hinchey	Democrat	27.2 points
2006	Maurice Hinchey	Democrat	17 points
2004	Maurice Hinchey	Democrat	24.8 points
2002	Maurice Hinchey	Democrat	24 points
2000	John Sweeney	Republican	30.8 points

Source: "New York's 22nd Congressional District," *Ballotpedia*, https://ballotpedia.org/New_York%27s_22nd_Congressional_District

Table 1.6 Recent NY-24 representatives

	Representative	Pavrty	Margin of victory
2016	John Katko	Republican	21.2 points
2014	John Katko	Republican	18.7 points
2012	Dan Maffei	Democrat	5.2 points
2010	Richard Hanna	Republican	5.9 points
2008	Michael Arcuri	Democrat	7.1 points
2006	Michael Arcuri	Democrat	6.7 points
2004	Sherwood Boehlert	Republican	15.9 points
2002	Sherwood Boehlert	Republican	Unopposed
2000	Sherwood Boehlert	Republican	41.9 points

Source: "New York's 22nd Congressional District," *Ballotpedia*, https://ballotpedia.org/New_York%27s_24th_Congressional_District

2016 Election

The 2016 election is an important backdrop for understanding how John Faso, Claudia Tenney, and John Katko approached the 2018 campaign, particularly given Faso and Tenney were freshman members of Congress.

County-level historical analysis demonstrates the power of the Donald Trump phenomena in Central New York in 2016. As seen in Table 1.7, Trump won five of the seven counties completely in NY-19 (Delaware, Greene, Otsego, Schoharie, and Sullivan) and three of four partially in the district (Broome, Montgomery, and Rensselaer). Trump flipped Sullivan County, which Barack Obama won comfortably twice, and Otsego County, where Obama narrowly won twice.

Table 1.7 County-level results for presidential elections in NY-19

	2008	2012	2016
Columbia	Obama +9	Obama +12	Clinton +5
Delaware	McCain +6	Romney +10	Trump +27
Greene	McCain +11	Romney +11	Trump +26
Otsego	Obama +4	Obama +2	Trump +11
Schoharie	McCain +13	Romney +17	Trump +33
Sullivan	Obama +8	Obama +10	Trump +11
Ulster	Obama +23	Obama +22	Clinton +11
Broome (partial)	Obama +13	Obama +5	Trump +2
Dutchess (partial)	Obama +13	Obama +7	Clinton (less than 1)
Montgomery (partial)	McCain +9	Romney +4	Trump +24
Rensselaer (partial)	Obama +8	Obama +12	Trump +1

Sources: "New York Results," *The New York Times*, August 1, 2017, https://www.nytimes.com/elections/2016/results/new-york; "New York; Election Results 2012," *The New York Times*, https://www.nytimes.com/elections/2012/results/states/new-york.html; "New York; Election Results 2008," *The New York Times*, https://www.nytimes.com/elections/2008/results/states/new-york.html

Table 1.8 Registered partisans in NY-19 (November 1, 2016)

	Democrats	*Republicans*	*Independents*	*Total*
Ulster	46,068	30,435	6637	126,288
Sullivan	20,463	14,150	2821	52,719
Columbia	14,891	12,704	3118	44,598
Otsego	11,733	13,983	2426	37,470
Greene	7985	12,757	2187	32,811
Delaware	8133	12,501	1806	29,443
Schoharie	5401	7943	1431	20,683

Source: "New York State Voter Enrollment by Assembly District," *The New York Board of Elections*, November 1, 2016, http://www.elections.ny.gov/NYSBOE/enrollment/assembly/assembly_nov16.pdf

Trump's victory in Sullivan County was particularly significant. As seen in Table 1.8, Democrats outnumber Republicans in the three most populated counties in NY-19. Sullivan County is the second most populated in the district, between Ulster, the most populated, and Columbia, the third most populated. Democrats had a 6313 registered voter advantage in Sullivan, which comprised 12 percent of the district's population. Hillary Clinton won Ulster and Columbia, as Obama did, but Clinton's vote share was less than Obama's.

Trump made substantial gains on Romney's 2012 performance in Schoharie, Greene, and Delaware counties. This was not surprising, given these counties are the most Republican in the district. At the same time, Trump's vote share illustrates how Republicans clearly identified more strongly with Trump's candidacy than Romney's.

John Faso was first elected to Congress in 2016 by defeating Zephyr Teachout 54.1 percent to 45.9 percent. Faso benefitted by portraying Teachout as a carper-bagger and "deftly distancing himself from presidential nominee Donald Trump."[16] Teachout, a law professor at Fordham University, made a name for herself in New York State politics by challenging Andrew Cuomo in the 2014 Democratic gubernatorial primary. Teachout moved to the district less than a year prior to Election Day. Polling between the candidates was virtually tied throughout the race until Faso opened a small lead in the final week.

Faso won every county in NY-19, full and partial, except for Ulster County. Hillary Clinton won Ulster County by nine points, her largest margin of victory in any NY-19 county. Faso won the other two counties Clinton carried: Columbia County and part of Dutchess County. In 2018, Antonio Delgado needed to swing these important counties back in a Democratic direction to be successful (Table 1.9).

Table 1.9 2016 Election results in NY-19

	Zephyr Teachout (D)	John Faso (R)	Winner	Presidency
Columbia	14,212	15,649	F +1437	Clinton +5
Delaware	6943	11,857	F +4914	Trump +26
Greene	7318	13,667	F +6349	Trump +25
Otsego	10,642	13,689	F +3047	Trump +11
Schoharie	4722	8733	F +4011	Trump +33
Sullivan	12,905	14,806	F +1901	Trump +9
Ulster	45,541	35,996	T +9545	Clinton +9
Broome (partial)	247	643	F +396	Trump +2
Dutchess (partial)	24,747	27,170	F +2423	Clinton +1
Montgomery (partial)	1581	3653	F +2072	Trump +24
Rensselaer (partial)	12,366	19,423	F +7057	Trump +1

Note: Vote tallies for Zephyr Teachout include the Democratic Party and Working Family Party ballot lines. Vote tallies for John Faso include the Republican Party, Conservative Party, and Independent Party ballot lines

Source: "Rep. in Congress Elections Returns," *The New York State Board of Elections*, November 8, 2016, https://www.elections.ny.gov/NYSBOE/elections/2016/General/2016Congress.pdf

Donald Trump won convincingly in each of the four counties completely within NY-22 (Chenango, Cortland, Madison, and Oneida). Republicans had a registered voter advantage in each, but Trump posted substantial gains compared to the two previous GOP presidential nominees, John McCain and Mitt Romney. Chenango County was home to the biggest leap for Trump, where he gained 21 points on Romney. The county was nearly 2 to 1 Republican. Trump also performed well in Oneida County, the most populated in the district and home to both Claudia Tenney and Anthony Brindisi, winning by 20 points. Barack Obama narrowly won Oneida County in 2008. Trump similarly dominated the four counties partially in the district (Broome, Herkimer, Oswego, and Tioga). Trump flipped Oswego and Broome counties, both of which voted for Obama twice.

Claudia Tenney was elected to Congress in 2016 by defeating Kim Myers 46.5 percent to 41.1 percent. Third party candidate Martin Babinec received 12.4 percent of the vote. Tenney previously undertook an unsuccessful Republican primary challenge to Richard Hanna in 2014, who retired in 2016. Tenney ran from the right, bolstered by the Tea Party, then Breitbart News. Hanna may not have been able to fend off another primary challenge from Tenney.

Tenney won every county but Broome, where Myers is from, and Cortland County, the most liberal rural county in the district, and home to a campus of the State University of New York. Myers struggled to generate sufficient support beyond her home base. Anthony Brindisi had deeper and broader appeal in 2018, given his experience as a New York Assemblyman from Utica, but also needed to maintain Myers' high level of support in Broome County to be successful. Trump's popularity in rural NY-22, particularly Herkimer County, Tioga County, and Chenango County, helped propel Tenney to large victories there. A Brindisi victory would require tightening these margins as well (Tables 1.10, 1.11, and 1.12).

Donald Trump won three of four counties located in NY-24. Hillary Clinton won Onondaga County, home to Syracuse, the most populated and sole Democratic county in the district. Clinton's vote total was less than Barack Obama's in both 2008 and 2012. Trump flipped Cayuga County, where Republicans narrowly outnumbered Democrats. Obama comfortably won Cayuga County twice. Oswego County, which his partially in NY-24, and went twice for Barack Obama, experienced a 30 point shift in Trump's favor.

Table 1.10 County-level results for presidential elections in NY-22

	2008	2012	2016
Chenango	McCain +2	Romney +3	Trump +25
Cortland	Obama +8	Obama +3	Trump +6
Madison	McCain +1	Obama (less than 1 percent)	Trump +14
Oneida	McCain +1	Romney +5	Trump +20
Broome (partial)	Obama +7	Obama +5	Trump +2
Herkimer (partial)	McCain +9	Romney +8	Trump +33
Oswego (partial)	Obama +2	Obama +8	Trump +22
Tioga (partial)	McCain +11	Romney +16	Trump +26

Sources: "New York Results," *The New York Times*, August 1, 2017, https://www.nytimes.com/elections/2016/results/new-york; "New York; Election Results 2012," *The New York Times*, https://www.nytimes.com/elections/2012/results/states/new-york.html; "New York; Election Results 2008," *The New York Times*, https://www.nytimes.com/elections/2008/results/states/new-york.html

Table 1.11 Registered partisans in NY-22 (November 1, 2016)

	Democrats	Republicans	Independents	Total
Oneida	49,389	52,662	8781	142,815
Madison	12,492	17,103	2979	44,772
Cortland	10,032	10,850	1848	31,807
Chenango	7953	13,230	1878	31,374

Source: "New York State Voter Enrollment by Assembly District," *The New York Board of Elections*, November 1, 2016, http://www.elections.ny.gov/NYSBOE/enrollment/assembly/assembly_nov16.pdf

John Katko was initially elected in 2014 by defeating incumbent Dan Maffei 59.9 percent to 40.1 and reelected in 2016 by defeating Colleen Deacon 60.6 percent to 39.4 percent. This was the first time NY-24 reelected an incumbent in a decade and the first Republican to win the seat during a presidential election year since 2004. Katko performed well outside of Syracuse, but also carried Onondaga County comfortably. This was remarkable considering Hillary Clinton's 14-point advantage in the district.

Successful appeals to independent voters are key factors in understanding Katko's electoral success. Katko "managed to hold onto the seat by positioning himself as a moderate Republican who voted independently and tried to work on bipartisan issues in Congress."[17] Katko considers bipartisanship his biggest legislative accomplishment in Congress. "Every district is different," Katko said, when asked about why he has proven to be more popular than neighboring GOP incumbents, but emphasized that he

Table 1.12 2016 Election results in NY-22

	Kim Myers (D)	Claudia Tenney (R)	Martin Babinec
Chenango	6989	10,170	1949
Cortland	9101	8249	1634
Madison	12,074	13,880	2533
Oneida	32,563	42,591	11,441
Broome (partial)	40,095	31,301	9981
Herkimer (partial)	5811	10,344	4993
Oswego (partial)	5759	10,244	1429
Tioga (partial)	1874	2665	678

Note: Vote tallies for Kim Myers include the Democratic Party and Working Family Party ballot lines. Vote tallies for Claudia Tenney include the Republican Party and the Conservative Party ballot lines. Vote tallies for Martin Babinec include the upstate Jobs Party and Reform Party ballot lines

Source: "Rep. in Congress Elections Returns," *The New York State Board of Elections*, November 8, 2016, https://www.elections.ny.gov/NYSBOE/elections/2016/General/2016Congress.pdf

	Winner (Myers vs. Tenney)	Presidency
Chenango	Tenney +3181	Trump +26
Cortland	Myers +852	Trump +6
Madison	Tenney +1806	Trump +14
Oneida	Tenney +10,228	Trump +19
Broome (partial)	Myers +8794	Trump +2
Herkimer (partial)	Tenney +4533	Trump +33
Oswego (partial)	Tenney +4485	Trump +22
Tioga (partial)	Tenney +791	Trump +26

Note: Vote tallies for Kim Myers include the Democratic Party and Working Family Party ballot lines. Vote tallies for Claudia Tenney include the Republican Party and the Conservative Party ballot lines

Source: "Rep. in Congress Elections Returns," *The New York State Board of Elections*, November 8, 2016, https://www.elections.ny.gov/NYSBOE/elections/2016/General/2016Congress.pdf

"spends an extraordinary amount of time with constituents" and believes he is "highly in tune with what my district wants."[18] Katko's perspectives on healthcare and the farm bill were cited as two relevant examples.

Though Katko represented a district where Democrats outnumbered Republicans, three of the four counties trended positively in a Republican direction in 2016. Wayne County voted more strongly for Trump than previous Republican nominees, while Cayuga County and Oswego County swung sharply right in 2016. Democratic challenger Dana Balter needed to do exceptionally well in Onondaga County, her geographic base, and similar to Brindisi in NY-22, considerably close the margins in rural counties (Tables 1.13, 1.14, and 1.15).

Table 1.13 County-level results for presidential elections in NY-24

	2008	2012	2016
Cayuga	Obama +8	Obama +11	Trump +12
Onondaga	Obama +19	Obama +21	Clinton +14
Wayne	McCain +11	Romney +9	Trump +25
Oswego (partial)	Obama +2	Obama +8	Trump +22

Sources: "New York Results," *The New York Times*, August 1, 2017, https://www.nytimes.com/elections/2016/results/new-york; "New York; Election Results 2012," *The New York Times*, https://www.nytimes.com/elections/2012/results/states/new-york.html; "New York; Election Results 2008, *The New York Times*, https://www.nytimes.com/elections/2008/results/states/new-york.html

Table 1.14 Registered partisans in NY-24 (November 1, 2016)

	Democrats	*Republicans*	*Independents*	*Total*
Onondaga	117,277	89,521	16,578	314,309
Wayne	14,431	23,297	3217	58,575
Cayuga	16,313	17,864	2797	49,943

Source: "New York State Voter Enrollment by Assembly District," *The New York Board of Elections*, November 1, 2016, http://www.elections.ny.gov/NYSBOE/enrollment/assembly/assembly_nov16.pdf

2016 Congressional Elections

Table 1.15 2016 election results in NY-24

	Colleen Deacon (D)	*John Katko (R)*	*Winner*	*Presidency*
Cayuga	10,712	21,511	K +10,799	Trump +11
Onondaga	87,118	117,230	K +30,112	Clinton +14
Wayne	11,898	25,753	K +13,855	Trump +25
Oswego (partial)	9312	18,267	K +8955	Trump +22

Note: Vote tallies for Colleen Deacon include the Democratic Party and Working Family Party ballot lines. Vote tallies for John Katko include the Republican Party, Conservative Party, Independent Party, and Reform Party ballot lines

Source: *The New York Board of Elections*, http://www.elections.ny.gov/EnrollmentAD.html

NOTES

1. Geoffrey Skelley, "Exit Stage Left or Right: Midterm Retirements and Open Seats in the House Between 1974 and 2018," *Sabato's Crystal Ball*, March 22, 2018, http://www.centerforpolitics.org/crystalball/articles/exit-stage-left-or-right-midterm-retirements-and-open-seats-in-the-u-s-house-from-1974-to-2018/
2. Steven Levitt and Catherine Wolfram, "Sources of Incumbency Advantage in the U.S. House," *Legislative Studies Quarterly*, 22.1 (February 1990): 45–60.
3. Jeffrey Jones, "Midterm Seat Loss Averages 37 for Unpopular Presidents," *Gallup*, September 12, 2018. https://news.gallup.com/poll/242093/midterm-seat-loss-averages-unpopular-presidents.aspx
4. David Schultz and Rafael Jacob, *Presidential Swing States*, Second Edition, Rowan and Littlefield: 2018.
5. Erik Engstrom, "Electoral Competition and Critical Elections," Chapter Six in *Partisan Gerrymandering and the Construction of American Democracy*, University of Michigan Press, 2013: 100.
6. "How *Five Thirty Eight's* House, Senate, and Governors Models Work," October 17, 2018, https://fivethirtyeight.com/methodology/how-fivethirtyeights-house-and-senate-models-work/
7. "Pivot Counties: The Counties that Voted Obama-Obama-Trump from 2008 to 2016," *Ballotpedia*, https://ballotpedia.org/Pivot_Counties:_The_counties_that_voted_Obama-Obama-Trump_from_2008-2016
8. "Pivot Counties: The Counties that Voted Obama-Obama-Trump from 2008 to 2016," *Ballotpedia*, https://ballotpedia.org/Pivot_Counties:_The_counties_that_voted_Obama-Obama-Trump_from_2008-2016
9. It is important to note that redistricting following the 2010 election reconfigured district boundaries.
10. This figure came from the Department of City Planning available at: https://www1.nyc.gov/site/planning/data-maps/nyc-population/population-facts.page
11. Geoff Herbert, "Gov. Cuomo says he's the 'voice' of upstate NY: 'I love upstate,'" *Syracuse.com*, November 21, 2018, https://www.syracuse.com/state/index.ssf/2018/11/cuomo_voice_upstate_ny.html
12. Christian Grose and Bruce Oppenheimer, "The Iraq War, Partisanship, and Candidate Attributes: Variation in Partisan Swing in U.S. House Elections," *Legislative Studies Quarterly*, 32.4 (November 2007), 531.
13. Luke Perry, "22nd Not as Republican As Tenney Claims," *Utica Center of Public Affairs and Election Research*, July 6, 2017. https://www.ucpublicaffairs.com/home/2017/7/6/ny-22-minute-22nd-not-as-republican-as-tenney-claims-by-luke-perry

14. It is important to recognize that the composition of NY-19, NY-22, and NY-24 changed significantly after the 2010 redistricting. All representatives for each district are listed throughout this century, but comparison before and after 2010 has limited utility.
15. Luke Perry, "NY-22 Minute: 2018 and 2014 Two Very Different Midterms for New York," *The Utica College Center of Public Affairs and Election Research,* December 25, 2018, https://www.ucpublicaffairs.com/home/2018/12/25/242eqlfrndvojxmm378aa8uekclof1
16. Matthew Hamilton and Rick Karlin, "Faso Defeats Teaching in $8.5 million race for NY-19," *Times Union,* November 9, 2016, https://www.timesunion.com/local/article/Faso-defeats-Teachout-in-8-5M-race-for-19th-10603303.php
17. Mark Weiner, "Katko beats Deacon; 1st incumbent in 10 years to win Syracuse's House Seat," *Syracuse.com,* November 9, 2016, https://www.syracuse.com/politics/index.ssf/2016/11/katko_beats_deacon_1st_incumbent_in_10_years_to_win_syracuses_house_seat.html
18. "John Katko Talks Campaign, Congress, Sessions and Trump with Luke Perry," *The Utica College Center of Public Affairs and Election Research,* September 12, 2018, https://www.ucpublicaffairs.com/home/2018/9/10/john-katko-ny-24-talks-congress-campaign-sessions-trump-with-luke-perry

CHAPTER 2

Issues and Messaging

Abstract This chapter examines key issues, tactics, and debates in the 2018 campaigns for NY-19, NY-22, and NY-24.

Keywords 2018 Midterm election • The Affordable Care Act • The American Health Care Act • The Tax Cuts and Jobs Act • Healthcare • Immigration • NY-19 • NY-22 • NY-24 • John Faso • Antonio Delgado • Claudia Tenney • Anthony Brindisi • John Katko • Dana Balter

Key Issues

There were two major issues in Central New York during the 2018 campaign, healthcare and tax policy. These issues touched on fundamental questions to U.S. politics, including the role of government in society and the allocation of finite resources. Both were domestic issues that impacted many citizens, had the ability to draw a sharp contrast between Republican incumbents and Democratic challengers, and invoked deep emotions.

Republicans campaigned to repeal the Affordable Care Act (ACA) since it was adopted in 2010. Unified government under the GOP, which began in 2017, was the best opportunity to deliver this promise. The House passed the American Health Care Act (AHCA) in May of 2017, which repealed the ACA. In August, the bill failed in the Senate, as John McCain memorably cast the decisive vote with an impassioned thumbs-down. Republicans regrouped and quickly shifted their focus to tax policy. Three months later the Tax Cuts and Jobs Act was passed. This was the major legislative accomplishment of the Trump presidency and the Republican-controlled Congress.

Healthcare

All three Central New York Republicans wanted to repeal the ACA. Claudia Tenney and John Faso voted for AHCA. John Katko voted against because the bill did not provide a viable replacement. Katko had long pledged not to repeal the ACA without a sufficient replacement that allows consumers to buy health insurances across stateliness, funds high-risk pools, implements tort reform, expands health savings accounts, and removes regulations preventing new prescription drugs from being more readily available.[1]

"Many of my Republican colleagues have the mantra of repeal-and-replace," Faso said. "That's never been my position. My position is keep what works and fix what doesn't."[2] In March of 2017, Faso stated that he would not support a new Republican healthcare bill unless certain portions of the ACA were preserved, including prohibitions against people with preexisting conditions and the ability for children to remain on their parents' health insurance plan until the age of 26. "I've met with many people across the district who like the ACA, who have gotten coverage for the first time or they previously had employer-based coverage (and) lost their job," Faso explained. "The ACA has been a Godsend to them. But I've met other people, particularly small business (owners) that have told me the ACA has discouraged employment," reduced coverage and increased the cost of deductibles.[3]

Behind the scenes, Faso was "a moderate voice in the contentious effort (among Republicans) to bring the far-right Freedom Caucus on board with 'repeal and replace.'"[4] For instance, a secret audio recording that went public included Faso encouraging Republicans to exclude a provision in the bill that defunded Planned Parenthood because of the political risks involved. Faso also negotiated an amendment with Chris Collins (R, NY-27) to end New York's practice of charging counties for 13 percent of Medicaid costs. Faso argued this would save local property taxpayers $358 million annually, while critics claimed this would endanger Medicaid coverage for New Yorkers and prompt the closing of nursing homes and healthcare facilities statewide.[5]

Faso referenced his work in the House Problem Solvers Caucus in presenting solutions for how to expand health insurance coverage and reduce the cost. For instance, Faso supported insuring insurance companies against losses resulting from costly customers who need a high level of care. Faso's proposal would have capped what insurers were responsible for per patient. The remaining cost would be covered by a government backed reinsurance program. Faso argued this would bring more predictability to the insurance market. Faso also supported raising the mandate on employers to provide insurance if they have 50 or more full-time employees to 500 or more employees. Faso believed the 50-employee threshold stifled economic development for small businesses. Faso became a crucial vote in moving the AHCA Act out of committee, which his political opponents relentlessly criticized.

Claudia Tenney's position on healthcare was a near universal rejection of the ACA, which she viewed as "devastating" for families and small businesses. Tenney believed the law was not working because of significant increases in the cost of premiums, deductibles, and co-pays, while "New Yorker's are losing their doctors." Tenney pledged to defund the ACA and "advocate for free-market, patient central healthcare."[6] She did vote to extend the Children's Health Insurance Program for ten years and claimed the AHCA protected people with preexisting conditions.

Tenney's public statements toward healthcare were largely focused on the perceived shortcomings of the existing system and generally aspirational toward Republicans developing a better alternative. "We're going to continue to fight the battle to do what we're doing—to give people a lifeline from Obamacare," Tenney explained in July of 2018. "We're also going to come up and try to renegotiate some kind of solution. … We're going to try to lower premiums. We're going to give people the opportunity to buy across state lines. Ultimately, we'd like to see us be able to repeal and replace Obamacare with something that actually gives quality health care, preserves the relationship between patients and doctors."[7]

Democrats deployed a concentrated, national strategy to focus on healthcare, which was on display in Central New York. Anthony Brindisi, Dana Balter, and Antonio Delgado all criticized their opponents for not sufficiently protecting people with preexisting conditions and damaging the ACA by undermining certain components, like removing the individual mandate. This criticism had traction, particularly against Tenney and Faso, who voted for repeal, by putting them constantly on the defensive and depicting their policy position as inhumane. Brindisi, for instance, described efforts to repeal the ACA as "heartless," borrowing a description by President Trump of one related bill, though the president supported repeal.[8]

At the same time, Democratic challengers differed on what the next step for healthcare should be. Balter supported a transition to "Medicare-for-All," a position Brindisi and Delgado sought to distance themselves from as their opponents sought to define them that way. Delgado and Brindisi both advocated for lowering prescription drug prices by letting Medicare negotiate with drug companies. Delgado supported a public option where anyone could opt into Medicare. Brindisi's position was more complicated. As Assemblyman, Brindisi voted for the New York Health Act, a failed bill that would have created a statewide universal payer system. Brindisi sought to defend that vote without advocating for universal healthcare at the national level. This was done through an appeal to federalism—what is best for one state, like New York, is not best for all 50 states.[9] These efforts were complicated by Brindisi's assertion that healthcare is a right. Brindisi never explained why all Americans are not entitled to healthcare if it is a right, and not just those who happen to live under states with universal health insurance coverage. Tenney missed a tactical opportunity by not pushing this conversation. Brindisi was vulnerable on this front in shifting from a liberal Assembly district to a conservative House district.

Tax Cuts

Republicans sought to shift from defense to offense in moving from healthcare legislation to tax policy. Many House incumbents, including Tenney and Katko, ran on the Tax Cuts and Job Act. They touted the perceived benefits to individuals, receiving more money in their paychecks, and to the economy, which experienced growth levels over 4 percent, and employment, which was lower than normal.

Tenney and Katko depicted the bill as a needed response to an unacceptable status quo. Tenney explained:

> Tax reform is the key to unleashing the American Dream for all. Our current tax code is broken and riddled with loopholes that penalize success and hurt hardworking taxpayers. This changes today. The passage of the Tax Cuts and Jobs Act will provide critical relief to individuals and families while ensuring that job creators in the 22nd District can compete on a level playing

field. Our tax code will now reflect the values of fairness and hard work. Without these tax cuts, our economy will continue to be stagnant and American competitiveness will continue to suffer.[10]

Similarly, Katko viewed the law as "the first major reform to our nation's tax code in three decades." He believed the bill helped American workers, delivered tax relief for local families, and helped local businesses invest, spurring economic growth. Katko highlighted how the law doubled the standard deduction, lowered individual rates, expanded the Child Tax Credit, and preserved the local property and income tax deduction. Katko explained:

> Despite the heated rhetoric surrounding passage of this legislation, the fact is that the status quo is simply not working for Central New York. Passage of this bill gives us a rare opportunity to level the playing field and put American workers first. I have always fought in the best interest of my constituents. I soundly believe this bill will deliver tax relief for Central New York families and allow local businesses to invest in our workforce. With the passage of this bill today, I'm excited to see our local economy grow and thrive.[11]

In contrast to healthcare, Tenney defended the bill with great policy detail. She argued "the typical American family making $73,000 will see a tax cut of $2,059," and "a family with two children earning $52,967, the median household income in the 22nd District, would save $1,458, while a single filer with one child and an income of $30,000 would save $834."[12] Moreover, Tenney contended that "in the 22nd District, where 99 percent of itemizers deduct less than $10,000 in property taxes, this provision will cover the overwhelming majority of property owners who own homes that are less than $450,000 in value." Tenney believed Albany was to blame for unfunded mandates and increased property taxes, and cited data that all eight counties she represented were among the highest taxed in the nation (measured by the ratio of property tax to home value) despite being far from wealthy.

John Faso voted against the bill because of the cap placed on the State and Local Tax Deduction (SALT). The SALT cap was a hot topic in New York, though it is unclear how electorally impactful this was. Faso believed the newly adopted cap was unfair, given how high taxes were in New York State. Faso explained:

I remain concerned that as a result of the state's high income and property taxes, the partial elimination of the SALT deduction effective January 1, 2018 impacts New York families more severely than those in other states. These families have already made financial decisions based on this deduction, and to have it removed without any chance to prepare, is unfair.

It's important to recognize that this bill does make positive changes in our tax code that will help American businesses of all sizes and their workers compete in the global economy. In addition, there will be many families and small businesses in the 19th district that will receive a tax cut under this legislation. However, the overall impact of changes to the SALT deduction will accelerate the trend of hardworking individuals and businesses already leaving our state—further eroding New York's tax base.[13]

Faso represented a more affluent constituency than Katko and Tenney, which meant higher federal tax liability, particularly as SALT was reduced. Still, Katko and Tenney faced many questions about how a SALT cap benefited constituents in New York. Both framed their response around the notion that they were instrumental in protecting SALT. For example, Tenney explained:

I fought an uphill battle to include provisions facing elimination that are vital to seniors, single parents, struggling families and overly burdened job creators throughout the debate on tax reform. Last week, I urged House and Senate leadership to retain the deductibility of up to $10,000 of property taxes, the federal Historic Tax Credit (HTC), and provisions allowing for the deductibility of medical expenses. Despite the fact that these provisions faced the very real threat of elimination and were not included in the original bill, my efforts were ultimately successful in securing the Historic Tax Credit, expanding the SALT deduction, and continuing the deductibility of medical expenses, to assist our most vulnerable seniors in defraying high medial costs.[14]

Architects of the tax bill wanted to reduce the public cost of the tax cuts, which the Congressional Budget Office later projected to be a deficit increase of $1.9 trillion over ten years.[15] Republican leaders first sought to eliminate SALT, so that taxpayers in high-tax states would generate more federal revenue, then agreed to a cap instead. Katko and Tenney did successfully help advocate for this, but were unable to erase the criticism of why anyone from New York would support legislation that disproportionately hurt New York taxpayers in the first place. Most of the New York

Congressional delegation was Democratic, so the political cost was minimal to Republicans statewide, but a factor in tight races.

The SALT cap was a portion of Democratic criticism of the Tax Cuts and Jobs Act, but not the major focus. Candidates, such as Antonio Delgado, claimed the "cap was used to pay for everything wrong in the bill."[16] Challengers heavily framed the tax bill in terms of economic populism, contending that corporations benefited most at the expense of citizens at large. All three expressed their general support for tax cuts, provided they were given to the people who needed them most. As Delgado explained:

> Working people pay enough taxes. America's tax policies should put working families and the middle class first, not the super-rich and large corporations. I vehemently oppose the proposed tax policies of President Trump and John Faso, and any other policy that funnels tax dollars from the middle class to billionaires and contributes to an already exploding federal debt.[17]

Democratic challengers explicitly rejected trickle-down economics. "The truth is," Brindisi contended, "that only 4 percent of the workers at Fortune 500 companies saw their wages increase after the tax bill. These corporations are using the extra money to buy back shares to enrich their shareholders."[18] Delgado described this as "massive giveaways to wealthy corporations" that never trickles down, limiting public spending on important priorities, such as education and social programs.[19]

All three candidates claimed that over 80 percent of the benefits go to the top of the economic ladder, which was "backward," as Dana Balter put it, considering the best way to grow the economy is from the inside out. Challengers also emphasized how the law increased federal debt and questioned what happened to the conservative principle of fiscal responsibility.

Republicans also faced some inherent challenges in running on a tax cut. While "tax cuts are considered a bedrock issue for Republicans that helps turn out base voters in off-year elections when participation is low," the law was passed "11 months in advance of a congressional election without taking the time to build public support," suggesting "Republicans may have seriously miscalculated."[20] Tax cuts were modest for middle income voters, $20 week on average, and Americans are typically unaware and/or forgetful of tax cuts anyhow. For instance, just one in five voters remembered receiving the federal tax cut under George W. Bush, when nearly 75 percent received one.[21] Less than 2 percent of voters in 2018 identified taxes as the most pressing national issue when the law was being adopted.

Negative Attacks

Race

There were several negative attacks and ads that generated controversy in NY-19, NY-22, and NY-24. The most prolific was in NY-19, which drew national attention. The National Republican Congressional Committee (NRCC) ran an ad entitled "Who am I?" The advertisement mashed clips of Delgado's campaign commercials with snippets of lyrics from his rap career. Some of the lyrics were graphic, including "Gotcha sweatin this like your havin sex to a porno flick," "God Bless Iraq," and use of the "N-word." This was one of several race-related ads run on behalf of vulnerable House Republicans in New York.[22]

The editorial board of *The New York Times* denounced the ad as "race-baiting" and questioned the notion that once being a rapper was disqualifying to run for Congress. The op-ed also took exception to Faso's statement that "Mr. Delgado's lyrics are offensive, troubling, and inconsistent with the views of the people of the 19th District and America."[23] The board believed Delgado was a "a strong candidate who has focused on preserving health care coverage, bringing more jobs to the region, protecting the environment and defending a woman's right to choose," making "an impressive case for being elected." Faso "has abandoned any effort to explain how he'd serve constituents, instead hoping that his quisling behavior toward the president and a cynical campaign of race-baiting will be enough."

Faso responded to *The New York Times* with a letter-to-the-editor that described their commentary as an "outrageous smear."[24] Faso believed Delgado was "obligated to explain what he meant by the songs he wrote, which denigrated our nation and the free enterprise system, and often glorified pornography and drug use," not that being a rapper disqualified him for public office. Faso also took exception to "many phrases derogatory to women and law enforcement," and questioned what the board "would say about me had I uttered the same words as my opponent has." Faso concluded the piece was "willfully misleading."

The ad was arguably unhelpful to both candidates. Faso was not responsible for the ad, but became entangled once he chose to defend the contents. This required Faso to publicly recognize and disavow racist support of his candidacy, while he modestly benefited from his opponent being defined as a "black rapper" among a small portion of the district. Delgado had to continually answer questions about a short-lived career he had little interest or benefit in discussing. NY-19 had the fourth highest percentage of "non-Hispanic whites" (85 percent) among the top 25 battleground districts, trailing only OH-12 (86 percent), NY-22 (88 percent), and IA-01 (89 percent).[25]

News Media

Attacks on news media were a frequent campaign tactic employed by Claudia Tenney in NY-22. Tenney criticized the *Observer Dispatch* (OD), Utica's 200-year-old daily newspaper, for its digital management of stories, alleging without evidence they removed stories from their website that portrayed Anthony Brindisi unfavorably. Tenney reflected President Trump's unique media approach, sustained attacks on news outlets coupled with attempts to make media-based appeals when politically beneficial, and an overarching desire for media validation. In short, Tenney regularly attacked the messenger as well as the message.[26]

Tenney had long been a critic of the news media, which she believed was not fulfilling its role as the fourth estate. In contrast, Tenney claimed to run her family pennysaver newspaper "honorably" as "an alternative to the media we had out there," particularly mainstream media, which she described as "hyperpartisan" and "very left leaning."[27] In March of 2018, Tenney claimed "the single biggest destructive force in our country is the media."[28] In June of 2018, she stated that one of President Trump's "greatest achievements" was "calling out" the news media, who "need to be a watchdog" and "need to be as independent as they can be."[29] Trump described the news media as an "enemy of the American people" after taking office and frequently attacked them during the first two years of his presidency.[30]

In July of 2018, Tenney's campaign began a social media series on Twitter and Facebook entitled "Fact Check Friday" to "set the record straight" when "the media fails to cover our wins of NY-22." "It seems like every day," Claudia Tenney for Congress stated in June, "there are biased, misleading reports."[31] OD reporters were the primary targets of the series.[32] Tenney was "just appalled" by how the OD covered the region, and claimed the paper was "instrumental in causing a lot of the decline in our community by not telling the truth to a lot of our residents here." "They seem to be in bed with the politicians that are in power," Tenney explained, "instead of really kind of calling them out."[33]

The OD editorial board was occasionally critical of Tenney, while the news section regularly reported on what Tenney was doing, often with direct statements from her and/or related press releases by her staff.[34] Reporters Greg Mason and Samantha Madison spoke with her multiple times during the campaign.[35] In January of 2018, for instance, Mason asked, "[W]hat do you think were some of your key accomplishments this year?" The *Observer Dispatch* printed her response:

> I think one of the biggest issues for us—even though there was a lot not to like about the health care bill—I think getting started on it or getting the conversation going on it is, to me, probably the most controversial, but is one of the most important things because it's just been a huge problem for our small business community and for individuals. Unfortunately, the Senate couldn't follow through. They couldn't come up with something that was going to happen for us, so we had to go to the next thing, which was tax reform.[36]

Tenney's media criticism during the campaign sought to deflect blame, evoke a popular foil, and ingratiate herself with Trump supporters. Most Americans felt exhausted by the amount of news being disseminated, a sentiment more pronounced among Republicans than Democrats.[37] Most Americans also believed the news media was fulfilling its role of government watchdog and "keeps political leaders from doing things that shouldn't be done," though Republicans were half as likely to believe this as Democrats."[38] At the same time, alienating moderate Republicans and independents, who tend to look more favorably toward the news media, was a major strategic risk with this approach.

Family

Tenney attacked Brindisi's family at the outset of the campaign in an interview with *USA Today*. In July of 2017, days before Brindisi declared, Tenney made "an issue of his father's 'notorious' background as a lawyer who decades ago represented defendants with ties to organized crime."[39] Tenney contrasted her father, John Tenney, a former New York State Supreme Court Judge, and Brindisi's father, stating:

He fought for law and order and Anthony's father represented some of the worst criminals in our community. You have to question ... some of things that have happened in his family. The voters make that decision. I'm not saying Anthony is part of any of that but that's the family you come from.[40]

When Tenney was asked if she believed this was significant, she replied:

The issue is about where you come from. His background is significant. I can't tell you how many people have come up to me in my community and said, 'Wow, I don't feel comfortable about some of the background that he has.'[41]

Ellen Foster, Brindisi's campaign manager, responded to Tenney's comments:

Because Congresswoman Tenney can't defend her disastrous record on healthcare, jobs and public education, she is resorting to attacking someone who won't even be on the ballot—and it's clear she already thinks she's behind. Anthony Brindisi believes that name calling never created a job in Upstate New York. And if personal attacks are the only play in Claudia Tenney's playbook, she will lose this election.[42]

Tenney did not mention Brindisi's family for over a year till resurrecting the issue in September of 2018 for a *New York Post* story.[43] A campaign memo, issued by Tim Edson, a longtime political consultant for Tenney, and prominent figure in her 2018 campaign, warned staffers of security risks posed by Brindisi's family, who were described as "criminal" and "thuggish." The memo stated:

Brindisi's family has used their political connections to get away with violence, intimidation and thuggish behavior for years. As the Brindisi family watches Anthony's political career end, they may return to what they know—violence and intimidation.

The memo advised staffers to "not go out at night alone," to "be aware of strange cars," to "be alert to whether you are being followed," and "examine your locks" for tampering. Brindisi's father and brother were cited as the source of concern.

Tenney stated in a related interview that she had a "good relationship" with Anthony and did not blame him for his family. Rather, she blamed higher educational institutions. "This is rural upstate New York, which is usually kind of a quiet place," Tenney said. "But I have 11 colleges in my district and that's where most of these people (troublemakers) are coming from."[44]

Louis Brindisi, Anthony Brindisi's father, was a criminal defense attorney, who at one time represented individuals believed to be involved with organized crime, and who pled guilty to possession of cocaine in 1991.[45] Louis stated that he stopped practicing criminal law in 1983, when his partner was murdered in their law office. Louis was out of his office that day because his wife died of cancer. Anthony was five years old. Louis subsequently denied being a mobster or a drug dealer.

Andrew Brindisi, Anthony's brother, was indicted for second-degree assault and leaving the scene of a personal injury accident after allegedly hitting a man, John Linen, with his car while driving in Utica in 2014. Linen acknowledged being intoxicated and standing in the road as Brindisi's car approached. He believed Brindisi was trying to kill him after trying to confront him about allegedly taking pictures of homes and residents in his neighborhood.[46] Brindisi claimed it was self-defense.[47] Brindisi, who was a Utica employee at the time, was sentenced to one-year probation, points on his license, and a $500 fine.[48]

Tenney sought to contrast this behavior with her own behavior. "Look at what the father has been charged with and somehow has been able to get out of," Tenney explained. "I've never even had a speeding ticket." She stated:

> His brother three years ago was charged with running over a guy. … It was caught on a camera and many police have said this should have been attempted murder. It was not. And he kept his job in the city of Utica and his father gave big donations to the city's mayor. … Can you imagine if someone in my family ran over somebody?[49]

Tenney's tactics were criticized by the editorial board of the OD, who described them as "a move right out of the Trump playbook—crass and tasteless, a shameful embarrassment to people on both sides of the political aisle who deserve a campaign focused on issues, not personal attacks on family members." This "classless assault" on Anthony Brindisi, "a man whose character is defined by honor, integrity, and respectability," was "yet another pathetic attempt to disparage a man whose entire public career—first as a member of the Utica school board and later as a member of the New York state Assembly—is defined by dignity and respect."[50]

Local political leaders echoed this sentiment, including several Republicans. Anthony Picente, Oneida County Executive, said Tenney's comments "were absurd, bigoted, and shameful yet wholly unsurprising." Picente stated:

> She (Tenney) has long-attacked people personally with no basis in fact and steeped in bizarre conspiracy theories throughout her numerous political campaigns. That is not what politics and government should be about. Campaigns should be about how candidates are going to move the community forward and in the case of Congress, how they are going to fix a system in Washington that can't get anything done. Anyone who knows Anthony Brindisi knows he is a man of integrity and honesty who believes in this community.[51]

New York State Senator Joseph Griffo, a Republican representing Utica and Rome, was mostly silent regarding the NY-22 campaign. Griffo, who worked closely with Brindisi in the state legislature, was recruited to run in 2016 by the National Republican Congressional Committee, but declined. Griffo issued the statement below, following Tenney's comments:

> Italian Americans are honorable, hardworking people who have made, and continue to make, meaningful contributions to America's greatness. Disparaging stereotypes are disappointing and unnecessary. Campaigns should focus on policy positions and the philosophical differences between the candidates and not on personal attacks.[52]

The mayors of Utica, Democrat Robert Palmieri, and Rome, Republican Jacqueline Izzo, expressed similar concerns. Izzo believed families should be off limits in campaigns. Palmieri believed that the community would benefit by greater focus on issues rather than personal attacks.

This line of attack appealed to NY-22 constituents who were die-hard Tenney supporters and already determined to vote for her. This was old news for others, who did not hold Anthony responsible for the actions of siblings or parents, raising questions of whether Tenney's actions were inappropriate and distasteful.

Integrity

John Katko's campaign ran a controversial ad about Balter's residency and tax liability. The ad portrayed Balter as a "visiting professor" who lived lavishly in Naples, Florida, "the land of sunshine and expensive homes," but failed to properly pay her taxes. "Dana Balter didn't pay her taxes in Florida," the ad stated, and "wants to raise our taxes here." Fact checking by *Syracuse.com* determined the ad misrepresented the situation. Balter lived in a condominium owned by her brother, not the pool clubhouse shown in the ad, or a "mansion," as suggested separately by Katko's campaign manager. The ad also failed to mention that Balter was contesting a sales and use tax bill related to her design business, which ultimately led to her being responsible for $47.29 and resulted in her paying $111.08 with the late fee.[53]

When asked about the ad, Katko contended Balter was "repeatedly dishonest about how long she's lived here, and what she was doing while out of town."[54] Balter claimed to make Syracuse her home 15 years prior, an assertion Katko questioned. The Balter campaign provided a timeline of when she lived in Syracuse. Balter moved to the region in 2003 to enroll at Syracuse University. In 2004 she suffered a head injury that created prolonged complications. Balter lived with her sister in Pennsylvania from 2007 to 2010 and then with her brother in Florida from 2010 to 2012. She returned in 2013, reenrolled at the university, and lived in the area since.

Katko's criticism of Balter's residency was a tactic he employed in beating Democratic incumbent Dan Maffei in 2014. Katko regularly cast doubt on Maffei's connection to Central New York and once quipped the only district Maffei cared about was the District of Columbia.[55] John Faso and Antonio Delgado sparred over residency as well. Delgado stated that he and his wife were born and raised in the district. Both left to pursue professional opportunities after high school, when Delgado said Faso moved to the district from Long Island. Faso criticized Delgado for living his entire adult life outside of the district and returning to run for Congress. In contrast, Faso emphasized how he lived in the district for 35 years and raised his family there.

Faso's criticism mirrored earlier attacks on Zephyr Teachout in 2016. Faso claimed Teachout was a "nice person, but she just dropped in here from Brooklyn and registered to vote in January," so "she's never voted in a general election in this district," and "has no connection to the people or the communities," nor any "civic or charitable or other business connection to this district."⁵⁶

Balter launched integrity-based attacks of her own, questioning the relationship of Katko's legislative behavior in relation to campaign contributions. For instance, Balter alleged that Katko "changed one of the major provisions of your own bill in the way that the airline industry wanted it to be changed" after receiving "thousands of dollars in contributions from the airline industry."⁵⁷ Katko's campaign described the allegation as "a grave, slanderous, and entirely unsubstantiated claim" that suggested he "illegally allowed a campaign contribution to influence a vote before the House Homeland Security Committee." Katko claimed the amendment in question was offered by a Democrat and supported by him in a bipartisan effort:

> Dana Balter's political extremism has reached a point that she is now attacking members of her own party for engaging in constructive, bipartisan legislating. If Dana Balter's hard-left extremism wasn't disqualifying enough, her willingness to engage in an outright lie and dirty trick like this certainly is.⁵⁸

Balter subsequently questioned why Katko voted to block the Internal Revenue Service's request for outside counsel in their auditing of Microsoft in 2015 before receiving campaign contributions from Microsoft and related lobbyists. Balter contended Microsoft stashed money abroad to avoid paying taxes on it. Katko said Balter was impugning his integrity. "You don't need to do this to get elected," Katko stated. He believed voters were intelligent enough to see through this and highlighted being appointed top federal prosecutor by three presidents, two of whom were Democrats, which would not have happened if his integrity was in question. Balter claimed to be explaining the facts to voters, who were curious about his actions, and have the right to know who their elected representatives are working for.

While Anthony Brindisi and Antonio Delgado regularly questioned the potential influence of corporate campaign contributions, Balter did so with the greatest depth and specificity. Balter also chose to launch these attacks in the context of the debates. Katko displayed effective communication skills, but political debates were not necessarily his strength. Katko was clearly surprised and upset by this line of questioning and unequivocally defended himself. This type of appeal had the most traction with liberal economic populists, who were already going to vote for Balter. Independents and moderates of both parties, who were familiar with Katko previous two Congressional terms, were much less likely to be impacted.

The Debates

Debates generate significant attention in the context of any campaign. Campaign operatives tend to dislike them because there is much to be lost and comparatively little to be gained for candidates, particularly for those in the lead. The primary goal is to avoid mistakes. This tends to produce heavily scripted responses to questions, nearly all of which are expected by candidates. For this reason, interestingly enough, the contents of debates are very useful in illustrating the frames, themes, and positions purposively adopted by candidates. They also provide opportunities for citizens and analysts to watch and hear candidates interact in real time, a rarity in American campaigns.

NY-19

Four debates in NY-19 were held throughout October of 2018. The contents of the first two debates, for which video was publicly available, were included in this analysis. In the first debate, John Faso and Antonio Delgado debated at the WMHT studio in Troy on October 19, 2018. The two candidates debated for a second time three days later at WAMC in Albany along with Green Party candidate Steve Greenfield and independent candidate Diane Neal.[59] Four issues were discussed in both of these debates: the controversial NRCC campaign ad, healthcare, immigration, and gun policy.

NRCC Campaign Ad
The first question of both debates touched on the NRCC ad about Delgado's previous rap career. Delgado said the ad was "deeply unfortunate" and spoke to a "divisive" and "ugly" political climate "we have to get beyond" to solve problems. Faso acknowledged the ad was "provocative," while observing the ad was not his, and that his opponent's words, not his, were the ones in question. Faso rejected racism in all forms, including anyone who would vote for him on the basis of race.

During the second debate, Delgado claimed his rap career was mischaracterized and drew attention away from more important issues facing the district. Faso believed there was no basis to judge Delgado since he moved into the district and then immediately ran for Congress, a move Faso described as "arrogant." The "provocative ads" were in response to "provocative lyrics," Faso explained. Delgado still subscribed to these "very radical, far left views about the economy, about how wealth is created in our economy," and the solutions to the problems facing the district.

Greenfield did not believe Delgado's lyrics were relevant, instead pointing to the work history of Delgado and Faso as corporate lawyers. Greenfield was incensed that his teenage children had to be exposed to regular mailings at home depicting blonde-haired women clinging to blonde-haired children because a black man was running for Congress. Like Delgado, Greenfield called for Faso to denounce the ad. Neal agreed with Greenfield that Congress has too many lobbyists and lawyers. She had no problem with musicians being creative within their medium and thought Delgado should not be penalized for this.

Healthcare
Healthcare was a major topic in the debates. Delgado advocated for a public option to help ensure consistency of coverage if someone's job situation were to change. Delgado wanted to reduce the cost of premiums and deductibles and called for Medicare to have negotiating power with drug companies. Faso stated that national Democrats and Delgado want a single-payer system that would "destroy Medicare as we know it," cost $32 trillion over the next decade, and "double everyone's income taxes."

Delgado said he was going to fight against efforts to repeal the ACA. Delgado believed Faso's related vote weakened protections for people with preexisting conditions. Delgado contended this was the case, even in New York, who has state protections against this, because the bill allowed states to seek a waiver. Faso claimed Delgado was distorting his view. "I support protections for everyone with preexisting conditions," Faso stated.

In the second debate, Faso said the ACA works for some, but not others. Protecting people with preexisting conditions, keeping young adults on their parent's coverage into their twenties, and developing exchanges are elements of the law that work and should be maintained, while rising and unaffordable premiums do not work. Faso argued that Delgado really wanted a single-payer system, such as Medicare-for-All, which would be too costly and result in large tax increases. "If you think healthcare is expensive now," Faso explained, "wait till it's free."

Greenfield was propelled to run by a lack of advocacy for Medicare-for-All, which he believed was the most ethical and economically sound choice for healthcare reform. Neal criticized healthcare being a profit-based industry, though was not enthusiastic about Medicare-for-All. Neal believed that all people should have health insurance and this could be done in a fiscally sound manner that appealed to liberals and conservatives.

Delgado described Faso's characterization of his position on healthcare as "profoundly dishonest." Delgado advocated for the establishment of a public option so all people have access to healthcare. He also believed that Medicare should have negotiating power with "big pharma," in order to bring down healthcare costs, but this has not happened because of large campaign contributions to members of Congress, including Faso.

Immigration
Delgado argued there was a moral and economic imperative to "bring people out of the shadows in a human and compassionate way," provided they did not break the law. The "indecent conversation" surrounding immigration, as national leaders make xenophobic appeals, needs to be replaced by productive, bipartisan efforts. "We are a nation of immigrants," Faso replied, "but we are also a nation of laws." Faso highlighted bipartisan immigration bills he cosponsored, supported enforcing existing laws, and opposed sanctuary cities.

In the second debate, Neal contended that a path to citizenship for undocumented workers is necessary because of the importance of agriculture to the district. Protecting these workers would be beneficial for them and the farmers who depend on their labor. Greenfield also supported a path to citizenship because all immigrant workers are of equal value and should be protected.

Delgado believed the Trump administration worsened immigration challenges by threatening the use of the military at the Southern border rather than working diplomatically with Mexico to address the migrant caravan from Honduras. Delgado favored a clean Deferred Action for Childhood Arrivals (DACA) bill and DREAM (Development, Relief and Education for Alien Minors) Act untethered to other immigration reforms. Delgado also criticized

Faso for not rebuking the president's policy of family separation. Faso opposed family separation, which he believed was morally wrong and illegal, and blamed Democrats for not working with Republicans to resolve this issue. Faso hoped genuine reform could be accomplished post-election.

Gun Policy

Delgado expressed support for protecting gun rights, but as with any right, the Second Amendment has limits, including not being able to own automatic weapons. Delgado cited a "gun epidemic" that involved young people in danger, mass shootings, and women more likely to be a victim of gun violence in domestic abuse scenarios. "We solve this problem by not electing members who have taken money from the NRA," Delgado concluded, as Faso has done.

Faso pointed to his support for the Trump's administration approach on this issue, including banning bump stocks and "closing the loophole" within the military of not disclosing red flags that arise in background checks. Faso claimed to support the Second Amendment, while "Mr. Delgado is clear he does not." Faso highlighted the prevalence of gun sportsmen and women in the district and contended that new laws will not stop gun violence. Faso stated most gun violence occurs with illegal handguns and called for increased mandatory minimum sentences for people convicted of crimes involving firearms rather than imposing new burdens on gun owners who already abide by the law.

In the second debate, Greenfield advocated for treating the Second Amendment as written and prioritizing public safety. The latter would be favored by keeping "weapons of war" out of the hands of citizens. Neal supported gun rights so long as the exercise does not impede on her right to live. Neal called for a gun registry and universal background checks.

President Trump and Party Leadership

There were many questions raised in only one of the two NY-19 debates examined here. Several touched on the Trump presidency and party politics. Candidates were asked who they voted in 2016. John Faso voted for Gary Johnson and did not want to elaborate. Delgado voted for Hillary Clinton, primarily due to her experience, and believed Trump's comments about women were disqualifying.

Candidates were prompted to discuss their own qualifications for office. Delgado believed his diverse experiences, and not being a career politician, enabled him to serve working-class families and work across the aisle. Faso believed his record illuminated his qualifications, particularly his proven record of bipartisanship. Both he and Delgado emphasized their humble roots and various achievements throughout their adult life.

Candidates were asked about deepening political divisions in America. Faso greatly respected his opponent and anyone who disagrees with him. Faso highlighted meeting with thousands of constituents throughout the district. "I am constantly listening," Faso explained, because a representative's fundamental job is to listen to all viewpoints. "We have to show our kids that we can conduct our public affairs in a responsible and civil manner," Faso said. Delgado believed bridging the political divide was a challenge and cited engagement with diverse groups of people through his life as instrumental to understanding how to bring people together.

Political divisions manifested themselves around attitudes toward leadership and policy during the first two years of the Trump presidency. Trade, for instance, was one controversial policy area. Delgado advocated being more cooperative than adversarial because "reckless" behavior threatened stability and U.S. interests. Delgado credited President Trump for his efforts in renegotiating more favorable terms for the North American Free Trade Agreement (NAFTA). Faso said the administration played "hardball" with U.S. allies, which was "unconventional," yet helped produce "tremendous wins," including increased financial contributions to North Atlantic Treaty Organization (NATO) by its members and better milk pricing. Faso also recognized that small manufactures in the district were concerned about steel and aluminum tariffs.

House leadership was a prominent topic during the 2018 campaign. Faso supported Kevin McCarthy (CA-23) for Speaker of the House if Republicans retained the majority. Faso believed there was a clear choice between himself, who believes in the free market and a more restricted government, and Delgado, who wants an expanded role for government. Faso criticized Delgado for opposing Republican-supported community banking legislation and suggested he was aligned with Nancy Pelosi (CA-12) and Maxine Waters (CA-43) on financial regulation issues.

Delgado replied that he did not see Pelosi or Waters on stage that evening, but did see Paul Ryan come to the district to campaign for Faso as a "nice pat on the back for your deciding vote to rip healthcare from millions of people across the country." Delgado said when Speaker Ryan was asked why he came to the district to support Faso, Ryan responded, "he makes our majority work." Delgado believed not citing more desirable characteristics, such as effectively representing constituents, cooperation, or bipartisanship, "says a lot" about Faso.

Delgado said he did not pledge support for anyone as Speaker. Faso described this as "laughable." Nancy Pelosi will be Speaker if Democrats win and "her agenda is higher taxes and increased fiscal regulation that crush the upstate economy."

Impeachment of President Trump was also a topic that was raised. Faso did not think impeachment was warranted. While the president had been a "polarizing figure," Faso believed he worked with the other side, particularly on issues like opioids and mental health. Faso said his actions in Congress have sought to "tone down the volume," then described Democratic attacks on Judge Brett Kavanaugh, President Trump's second Supreme Court nominee, as a political assassination attempt and "the liberal version of McCarthyism," concluding "venom runs on both sides." Delgado noted the "ongoing investigation" by Robert Mueller, which was "very fruitful in a meaningful way," citing several guilty pleas. Delgado believed the investigation should be concluded before any determination is made about impeachment, though he did not share his opponent's view that the process is a "witch hunt."

Faso and Delgado agreed on some policy issues, such as the opioid crisis. Delgado appreciated Faso's work on the Synthetics Trafficking and Overdose Prevention Act (STOP Act), a 2018 law that sought to prevent opioids, such as fentanyl, from coming into the United States from abroad. Delgado thought more needed to be done, including increased drug treatment centers and programs. Faso generally agreed and highlighted increased funding for opioid treatment, prevention, education, and enforcement. There is "not a dime's worth of difference between Democrats and Republicans on this issue," Faso concluded. Delgado stated that pharmaceutical companies should be held more responsible for this crisis and cited his experiences visiting with parents who have lost children to opioid addiction. Faso believed that pharmaceutical companies should be held accountable if they violated the law.

The two candidates sparred on other policy issues, such as climate change and military spending. Faso acknowledged that human activity contributes to climate change, emphasized his work in the House bipartisan climate change caucus, and highlighted the importance of local companies in creating clean technologies in the private sector. Delgado criticized Faso's poor conservation record, particularly his professional and public connections with fossil fuel companies, which Delgado believed inhibited Faso's willingness to sufficiently support renewable forms of energy.

Delgado believed that militarization was being prioritized over sufficiently supporting the State Department. Military readiness was an important concern, but the government also needed to be smarter about allocating resources, so that newer threats, such as cybersecurity, were effectively addressed. Faso believed the sequester limited the U.S. government's ability to effectively fund the military and supported an audit of military spending to enhance efficiency and remove waste. "The price of liberty is not free," Faso stated, so the United States needs to ensure that the military is well trained and well equipped.

Current Events
Campaigns unfold in real time. Candidates are regularly questioned about current events, including during debates. A prominent example was the extraordinary confirmation hearings of Brett Kavanaugh, a federal district court judge who overcame accusations of sexual assault in narrowly being confirmed to the Supreme Court in a heavily partisan vote. Faso supported Justice Kavanaugh and claimed Democrats did not have "clean hands" in failing to abide by norms of fairness and rule of law. The sexual assault allegations were from 30 years ago and were thoroughly examined. Delgado believe that "this was a very difficult hearing for the country to endure" and opposed Kavanaugh's nomination prior to the hearings because his views were counter to abortion rights for women. Delgado criticized Faso for supporting Kavanaugh's confirmation after acknowledging allegations by Christine Blasey Ford were credible.

Sexual harassment policy for Congress was a related topic. Faso supported eliminating "hidden settlements" for cases of sexual harassment involving Congressional employees. Faso cited his mother's advice, "don't do anything you wouldn't want me to find out about," as sound advice for all. Delgado expressed concern about a "culture of gender inequity." Delgado referenced women not receiving equal pay for equal work, being in elevated danger for sexual assault on college campuses, and having their reproductive rights being curtailed, in advocating for federal policies to address these problems.

The prospect of legalizing recreational marijuana in New York State was a prominent issue in 2018. Delgado supported federal examination of legalizing medical marijuana and adult use. Faso did not support legalization and called for examining the effects on public safety, drug addiction, and academic performance among young people in states that have legalized marijuana. Faso criticized federal discriminatory practices toward companies who are legally in the marijuana business per state law. Both candidates supported federal funding of research on marijuana as a remedy for posttraumatic stress disorder.

Some current events touched on international affairs. Candidates were questioned about the death of Jamal Khashoggi, for instance, a Saudi national who resided in the United States and wrote for *The Washington Post*. Faso believed Khashoggi was murdered by Saudi security forces in Turkey and called for diplomatic pressure, including sanctions. Faso believed the U.S. should be mindful of the important relationship between the United States and Saudi Arabia, but made clear what happened was "completely unacceptable." Delgado agreed and called for a comprehensive reassessment of America's relationship with Saudi Arabia. Delgado also emphasized the important role the United States should play as a democracy protecting freedom of the press.

Delgado disagreed with the Trump administration unilaterally moving the capital to Jerusalem. This was not the best approach for the United States who portends to be a neutral arbiter in the Middle East. Delgado mentioned how his wife and children are Jewish. He considered himself pro-Israel as well as pro-democracy. Delgado said Israel was not a Jewish democracy, "settlements make it so that it can't be," and believed there needed to be a two state solution.

Faso described Israel as a strong and vibrant democracy, as well as America's main ally in the region. Faso believed moving the embassy was the right move and Delgado's view toward Israel was "dangerous," as was his perspective toward Iran, which Faso believed was a major security threat to the United States.

NY-22

There were three debates and/or forums in NY-22 with both candidates. These were spread out over the last month of the campaign and are discussed chronologically.

The First Forum

The first public forum was hosted by the Rome Chamber of Commerce on October 17, 2018. Each candidate was permitted to make opening and closing statements and answer questions posed by a moderator over one hour.

Both candidates emphasized what inspired them to run for Congress during their opening statements.[60] Anthony Brindisi discussed people he visited throughout the district and their concerns about paying bills and having health insurance. "These are the people I want to fight for in Washington," said Brindisi, who aspires "to bring people together to solve big problems." Claudia Tenney first ran for office because she "wanted to help the small business community" and for people to better understand how much small businesses contribute to communities in the district. Tenney aspired to reduce government and cut taxes to help businesses thrive.

Political attacks began with Tenney's response to the first question, which pertained to Defense Finance and Accounting Service (D-FAS) in Rome, a major federal government employer in the district. Tenney was critical of Senator Schumer's handling of related funding legislation. Brindisi contended the U.S. Senate put stronger language in the bill to protect workers. The two candidates exchanged barbs throughout, occasionally interrupting one another during her/his allotted time. One example was when Tenney responded to criticism of her efforts to repeal the ACA by stating the related bill did not pass. "Thank God," Brindisi quipped. Both repeatedly accused the other of lying, before an audience that included over 80 students from seven local high schools. At one point, for instance, Tenney accused Brindisi of producing a "word salad of lies," during a particularly testy discussion of immigration and Social Security, and later called him an "ambulance chasing trial lawyer."

Both candidates were comfortable and commanding in their own way. Tenney had clear talking points, but fluidly weaved between policy specifics on various issues and condemnation of Democratic leaders, the Resist movement, the news media, and various individuals from Ray Halbritter (described as the "biggest tax cheat") to George Soros (referred to as a "socialist").

Brindisi emphasized a collective to approach to governance, highlighting his work with Republicans, including Oneida County Executive Anthony Picente, Mayor Jacqueline Izzo of Rome, and New York State Senator Joseph Griffo. Brindisi referred to Griffo as his "biggest partner" in the New York Legislature and referenced former Congressman Sherry Boehlert (R) as a positive model for how to best represent the district today. This was done in concert with a policy focus on preserving the ACA and critiquing the Tax Cut and Jobs Act.

The forum was largely a contest of broad ideological values. Tenney depicted Brindisi as too liberal and a threat to conservative policy priorities regarding taxation and immigration. Brindisi depicted Tenney as too divisive and a threat to liberal policy priorities regarding expanding health insurance and protecting social programs, particularly Medicare and Social Security. Though both candidates opened and closed in personal terms—Tenney referenced living in the house across the street from where she grew up, while Brindisi referenced his political beginnings on the Utica School Board and what he's heard in town halls—the forum was more about what each stood for and the flaws in their opponent's views and actions.

Tenney framed her support for President Trump in terms of relationships and results. She suggested that her positive working relationship with the president was grounds for reelection, evident in visits to the district by him and Ivanka Trump. In speaking with reporters after the event, Tenney said with a smile, Trump listens to her, and is a good listener, though "he doesn't always listen for long."

Tax policy was emphasized as a key example of results. Tenney contended the federal tax cut was long overdue and responsible for positive developments regarding economic growth and employment. Brindisi contended the benefits of the tax law disproportionately favor the wealthy while significantly contributing to the federal debt. To address job loss upstate, Brindisi prioritized ensuring a pathway for young people from school to the local workforce, increased public works programs, and encouragement of emerging industries, such as renewable energy. Tenney emphasized her belief that government should not spend money to create jobs, the private sector should, and if the economy is growing, employment will rise.

Brindisi referenced select positions held by President Trump he agreed with while refraining from criticizing him directly. This tended to focus on proposals Trump campaigned on, such as an infrastructure bill and allowing Medicare to negotiate drug prices with pharmaceutical companies, but have yet to materialize. As previously mentioned, one clear parallel between Tenney and Trump in the forum was Tenney's treatment of the news media. Tenney criticized the local news media as "real fake news," gesturing at journalists in their designated space. Tenney then later offered video to media fact-checkers regarding Brindisi's past record on gun policy.

The Second Debate

The second debate was hosted by *Spectrum News* on October 25, 2018 at Colgate University. Several of the debate's topics echoed the first forum, including the economy, tax policy, and immigration. The dynamics of this debate were different as the panel, led by Liz Benjamin, host of *Capital Tonight*, asked follow-up questions, and attempted to establish clear responses.

There was more discussion of foreign policy in this debate, which provided some points of agreement. For instance, both candidates supported sanctions against Saudi Arabia in response to the murder of journalist Jamal Khashoggi. Both also would vote "yes" to the renegotiated NAFTA treaty and expressed mixed reviews for President Trump's pursuit of negotiations with North Korea.

Panelist Nina Moore, Chair of Government at Colgate University, pressed Tenney on her view toward Russian meddling in U.S. elections. Tenney initially contended everyone agreed that Russia meddled but "interfered in a minor way, we can't prove how much they've done." She emphasized that indicted Russians are unlikely to be prosecuted and suggested China poses a greater threat because they have more power, people, and money. When asked to clarify, Tenney explained that Russia unequivocally meddled, but believed this was separate from the unfounded assertion that President Trump colluded with Russia in pursuing the presidency. Brindisi was "very worried" about Russian meddling, believed Russia should be held accountable, including through sanctions, and provided some related policy suggestions, including nationalizing New York state requirements that sources of online advertisements be disclosed.

Exchanges were testy at times. For instance, a debate that began with a question about recent domestic bomb scares and dangerous political rhetoric saw both candidates (who condemned this behavior) spend the next hour attacking, interrupting, and speaking over one another, at times making it nearly impossible for the moderator to reestablish order. Tenney repeatedly sought to portray Brindisi as someone he claimed not to be—a Nancy Pelosi supporter who wanted to impeach Donald Trump. Brindisi stated he would neither support Pelosi for Speaker, nor vote to impeach President Trump. Brindisi matched Tenney blow-by-blow, relentlessly defending himself, as he saw it, from her attacks. Brindisi's supporters believed this was necessary to prevent Tenney from defining him; however, not all of Brindisi's attacks were retaliatory, and going negative posed risks as well, including triggering partisan cues prompting Republicans to unify around Tenney and/or turn off independents.

The Final Debate
Tenney and Brindisi debated for the final time on November 1, 2018, at WSKG studio in Vestal, which is located in the Southern portion of the district.[61] Tenney introduced herself as a life-long resident and small business owner. She claimed to stand up to corruption and touted her work on deregulation and lowering taxes, including for 95 percent of constituents. Tenney emphasized her relationships in Washington and bipartisan work, including how all the bills she sponsors has a Democratic cosponsor. Brindisi introduced himself through personal anecdotes of constituents he met at town halls and the challenges they face, including struggles regarding healthcare and family farming. Brindisi criticized Tenney for trying to repeal the ACA and supporting a tax cut benefiting the wealthy.

There were there five major policy topics raised: healthcare, gun policy, pocketbook issues, drug policy, and minority rights. Brindisi advocated for "stopping the assault on the ACA." Brindisi claimed 40,000 people in NY-22 would have lost their health insurance if the AHCA was passed. Two hundred and eighty-nine thousand constituents would have been in danger of losing coverage because they have preexisting conditions. Brindisi praised President Trump's campaign position that Medicare should be allowed to negotiate with drug companies, which Brindisi said would save $240 billion. Tenney claimed that the ACA was "imploding" and "destroying communities." The repeal effort was designed to save hospitals and people who are not getting healthcare because New Yorkers are paying "enormous amounts of money" for premiums and deductibles. Tenney cited her coauthorship of a bill that prohibited insurance companies from discriminating against people with preexisting conditions and called for the replacement of Obamacare by a patient-driven system, whereas Brindisi wanted Medicare-for-All. Brindisi believed the repeal of the individual mandate was responsible for rising premiums and cited how all NY-22 hospitals and AARP opposed the GOP repeal.

Discussion of gun policy focused on what should be done about gun violence. Tenney supported banning bump stocks, strengthening background checks, and working to reduce school violence. Tenney cited the Fix NICS (National Instant Criminal Background Check System) Act and STOP School Violence Act as examples of legislative progress. Brindisi said, "[W]e need to do everything we can to be respectful of people's Second Amendment rights, but also recognize we have an issue of gun violence in this country and we need some common sense reforms to try to cut down on gun violence." Brindisi supported expanded background checks. The biggest problem in New York, which has universal background checks, are guns purchased legally elsewhere and smuggled into the state. Brindisi called for this loophole to be changed and wanted to address other related considerations, such as better mental health evaluation and support. Brindisi did not support reinstating the federal assault weapons ban of 1994. Background checks were the best focus because there was the most agreement on this. Tenney claimed Brindisi was "so duplicitous on this issue" and claimed that Brindisi criticized the New York Safe Act and now wants to expand this law to be adopted nationally, which Brindisi denied. Tenney cited Brindisi's "F" rating from the National Rifle Association because he does not defend gun rights. Brindisi scored an "A" rating for several years as Assemblyman until his rating was changed shortly before Election Day.

When asked about how the candidates would address wealth inequality, Brindisi said he would start by never supporting a tax bill where 83 percent of the benefit went to wealthy individuals and companies. Brindisi expressed concern that wages were stagnated as people earned $4000 less than they were earning 16 years ago—a problem exacerbated by companies undertaking stock buybacks after the tax cut rather than raising wages. Tenney claimed that Brindisi was reading off talking points from Nancy Pelosi. Tenney visited nearly 50 businesses, none of whom failed to receive a tax cut, except for very wealthy individuals. Tenney stated that "tax and spend liberal policies" supported by Brindisi resulted in suffering and outward migration of people from the district.

Tenney contended that raising the minimum wage higher than surrounding states would be a big mistake. She claimed tax cuts were working creating an "employee's market." Wages were rising "naturally" and "organically" as they should, and not through onerous regulations. Brindisi stated that Tenney would know wages were not rising locally if she would have done town halls. Brindisi supported raising the minimum wage and establishing a living wage.

In regards to childcare, Tenney spoke of her experiences raising her son as a single mom and caring for her parents when they were ill. She referenced doubling the childcare credit and bringing Ivanka Trump to the district to discuss this issue. Brindisi viewed providing better childcare as a central consideration to addressing poverty. He supported increased federal government spending on childcare and related issues, like public transportation. Brindisi lauded the district's "great colleges and universities," while citing student loan debt as a top concern among college students. Providing refinancing options, lower interest rates, and increasing Pell grants would help address this. Brindisi described Betsy DeVos as the worst Secretary of Education ever and expressed concern about corporations profiting off college students because people on the Financial Services Committee, including Tenney, did not want to sufficiently regulate them. Tenney stated the country had failed to address the rising cost of higher education, citing the tuition cost of her alma mater, Colgate University. She claimed the federal government had already done much of what Brindisi called for, such as lowering interest rates and increasing Pell grants.

Opioid addition and marijuana legalization were two central themes related to discussion of drug policy. Tenney stated that approximately 115 NY-22 residents die annually from overdoses. The president, who Tenney believed "has been really a leader on this," devoted record funding to this problem. Tenney shared that two of her neighbors' children had died from opioid overdose, demonstrating how the issue knows no boundaries and constitutes a "tragedy of epic proportions." Brindisi agreed, but stated that repealing the ACA would have made the situation much worse. He called for greater investment in prevention and treatment, as well as going after drug companies and distributors who have taken advantage for people for far too long.

Brindisi believed the states should decide whether or not to legalize marijuana, not the federal government. Tenney expressed concern about addiction if recreational marijuana was legalized in New York. She personally attacked Brindisi by stating his "partner and mentor has had five felony drug trafficking charges" and pled guilty to a misdemeanor. Tenney also criticized Brindisi's family law firm for being hired by local governments to sue drug companies for their role in furthering opioid addiction. Tenney thought the latter should be done with no public expense. As previously discussed, Tenney attacked Brindisi's family on multiple occasions during the campaign. This was the first time she did so during a televised debate. "Shame on you" for the personal attacks, Brindisi replied, and then urged them to stick to the issues, and criticized Tenney's record of campaign donations from drug companies.

Tenney and Brindisi agreed when it came to questions on discrimination. For instance, Tenney said she was one of the few people who supported transgender people in the military and opposed the amendment that sought to prohibit them from serving. She believed this determination should be left up to Secretary of Defense Jim Mattis and be based on readiness. Brindisi applauded Tenney for her vote on that bill. In regards to representing African-Americans, Brindisi referenced holding many town halls in inner-city Utica "trying to reach out to voters wherever they are." Brindisi believed that criminal justice reform was a good start, followed by jobs programs, particularly for the inner city, to lift everyone up. Tenney said Brindisi was right that discrimination was still a problem and needed to be addressed. She said she will stand up for anyone who got "bullied and beat up" like she has as a woman in politics who takes on people with money and power.

Appeals to, and mobilization of, African-Americans was not a strong suit of the Brindisi campaign. There were few people of color in downtown Utica when Brindisi launched his campaign, even though he represented communities with large minority populations. Brindisi's debate response reflected a strong association with African-Americans to inner-city communities, crime, and unemployment. White Democratic candidates in the Central New York rust belt have long struggled to sufficiently connect with racial and ethnic minorities, most of whom are liberal, in ways that maximize turnout. This challenge is multifaceted, touching upon systemic racism, economic underdevelopment, educational disparities, urban planning, immigration tensions, political calculations, and much more. And one worthy of further examination because Democrats in predominately white, rural, conservative House districts cannot depend on suburban swing voters and white progressives to consistently win close elections.

Tenney closed by pointing to an "authentic, independent record" in the face of a "smear campaign" coming from the political left. She believed Brindisi had sided with "some of the richest and most powerful people," such as Ray Halbritter and Nancy Pelosi. Tenney did not believe Brindisi could be trusted, claiming he will vote for Pelosi as Speaker and oppose the president. Brindisi claimed that Tenney had to resort to "guilt by association" attacks because she had a failed record in Congress, aligning with corporate special interests. Eighty-five percent of Brindisi's donations came from individuals and his average contribution was $25. Brindisi said "the truth is I've always been independent" and pledged to support any good idea in Washington whether it came from a Democrat or a Republican.

NY-24

There were four NY-24 Congressional debates. The first debate was hosted by *Syracuse.com* on October 24, 2018.[62] The second debate, and the first to be televised, was hosted by *CNY Central* on October 30.[63] The third debate was hosted by *Spectrum News* on November 1 at Onondaga Community College. The final debate was held on November 4, just days prior to the election, and hosted by *WSYR NewsChannel 9* in Syracuse.[64] Video for the first, second, and final debates was publicly available. There were four issues that spanned all three of these debates: the economy, healthcare, immigration, and opioids.

Katko highlighted the lowest unemployment rate in 18 years, economic growth over 4 percent, and a growing stock market, as evidence of how the economy was performing well and exceeding expectations. Balter said "the country has been moving in the right direction for many years now" since President Obama's leadership pulled the country out of recession. "We are facing some difficult economic times," as Central New Yorkers continue to struggle to get by, even with increased economic growth. The tax cut increased economic inequality and benefitted the wealthiest at the expense of those who needed the most help. Balter also expressed concern over trade policy because of the negative impact of the trade war has on farmers in the district and the rollback of Dodd-Frank financial protections put in place to prevent another recession.

Katko said it was "absolutely not true" that 83 percent of the benefits go to the wealthiest Americans. This was only the case if the law sunsets. Katko claimed the tax cut would probably "pay for itself over ten years" if the economy continues to grow at 4 percent. Balter believed 4 percent growth was unlikely to persist all decade, making it "ridiculous" to think the tax cut will pay for itself.

In terms of healthcare, Katko emphasized his independence in opposing President Trump's efforts to repeal the ACA. Katko said protecting people with preexisting conditions and keeping people on their parents' insurance until the age of 26 were two of the great innovations of the ACA he would continue to support. Balter claimed Katko voted numerous times to restrict coverage for people with preexisting conditions. Katko defended his support for repealing the individual mandate because he believed it was unconstitutional, even though the Supreme Court disagreed.

Balter claimed "the tax cut gutted the ACA" and premiums were rising as a result. Katko believed Balter had a "very extreme" view on healthcare, Medicare-for-All, which "would destroy Medicare as we know it." Balter responded that Medicare-for-All would preserve Medicare and be cheaper than current healthcare costs. This was a "smart, economic approach," because the system would operate more efficiently and help all people be able to see a doctor when they needed to. Katko contended that Medicare-for-All would double the size of government and taxes overnight. Balter responded that arguing "the way to destroy Medicare is with more Medicare defies all logic." Both accused the other of "scare tactics" in discussing this issue.

In regards to immigration, Katko believed that the United States needed greater border security, citing experiences living and working along the border, and witnessing people regularly running across. He described the migrant caravan as a humanitarian crisis because "individuals are trying to find a better lives for their kids." At the same time, Katko said "we cannot have a revolving door at the border." Katko cited national security briefings he regularly received as a member of the Homeland Security Committee, including terrorist threats, drug trafficking, and human trafficking. Katko was unsure if a wall would be helpful, but believed that greater law enforcement presence was necessary.

Balter said there was no question the border needed to be controlled. Balter disavowed Katko's claim she wanted to abolish the Immigration and Customs Enforcement Agency (ICE) and referenced the American tradition of helping refugees. Balter emphasized how the people in the caravans were refugees fleeing violence and did not constitute an immediate threat of any kind. Balter believed President Trump's related rhetoric was stirring up fear a week before an election. Katko replied that fomenting fear is wrong, to the extent it was occurring, but also supported the president's efforts to better secure the border. Katko referenced a picture on Facebook where Balter participated in a protest with an "Abolish ICE" poster. Balter said the protest in question opposed the Trump administration's practice of child separation at the border, an issue she claimed Katko failed to address.

The two candidates agreed on one component of immigration—birthright citizenship. Katko disagreed with President Trump's contention he had the ability to overturn birthright citizenship. Even if a legal loophole was found, Katko contended, it would overturn over 200 years of relevant case law. Katko believed any change to birthright citizenship would have to be done through amending the constitution. Balter agreed with Katko that the president does not have the power to change birthright citizenship, nor should he.

Katko and Balter also largely agreed on combating opioid addiction. Katko emphasized his experience as a federal prosecutor of drug crimes. The challenge with heroin is how deadly it is. Katko believed stricter punishments would help deter heroin dealers. Balter echoed harsh punishments for heroin dealers, while emphasizing that drug addiction is a medical condition and should be treated as such. Balter believed the federal government should assist in expanding access to drug treatment centers, doctors, and medicine to help treat this illness. Katko agreed and was proud to "lead the charge" on federal spending toward drug treatment, citing the Comprehensive Addiction Recovery Act.

President Trump and Party Leadership
There were several issues raised in just one of the debates. Many pertained to the Trump presidency and party politics. National leadership was one key consideration. Katko wanted viewers to look at him carefully as he said "I'm not Donald Trump." Katko claimed his opponents say he voted with Trump 90 percent of the time, and "therefore I'm some kind of bad person and you must vote with her (Dana Balter)." Katko wanted the president to be successful, for the sake of the country, but like President Obama, Katko has supported and opposed presidents based on the merits of their actions. Katko also emphasized that he is one of the most bipartisan members of Congress.

For Balter, Trump is a central concern to some voters, not others. Balter tried to focus on how developments at the national level impact people in Central and Western New York, such as trade policy. Balter believed it was very important for Democrats to provide a check on the president, no matter who is president. Balter believed Republicans failed to uphold this responsibility and NY-24 constituents suffered for it. Katko claimed the current Congress was "one of the most productive in recent memory" with direct local benefits, including the lowest unemployment level in Central New York in years. Katko contended that the Senate inherently provides a check on the president, as well as the House, because 60 votes are needed to pass any legislation. "Put aside whether you like the president's personality and his tweets," Katko concluded, "we're producing."

When asked to grade the president's performance, Katko gave him a "B," and Balter an "F." Both candidates would not make any decisions regarding impeachment until the results of the Mueller investigation were in. Both also believed the Mueller investigation should end only when Robert Mueller determined that his work was concluded. Katko believed Brett Kavanaugh should be a Supreme Court Justice; Balter did not. Katko said he would vote for Kevin McCarthy for Speaker of the House if he agreed to change the rules as the bipartisan Problem Solvers Caucus called for. Balter said she would make that decision after knowing who was running and had an opportunity to evaluate the candidates.[65]

Several questions addressed the candidates' motivation for running for Congress and how they would appeal to voters. Balter "was not primarily running against President Trump." Rather, she ran on her vision for the country and Central and Western New York, as a place where everybody has opportunity and access to good paying jobs, adequate healthcare, and the environment and natural resources are protected.

"Oh, my lord," Katko replied, when asked a modified version of the same question with particular emphasis on why he has not stood up more to President Trump. Katko questioned how anyone could stand up to him more. Katko believed it took courage for him to vote for Nikki Haley in 2016, not Trump, and subsequently stand up to the president "time and time again." According to Katko, this included "hammering" Trump on his claim there was no Russian meddling in the 2016 election, routinely defending the Mueller investigation, and bucking the president with his legislative efforts regarding the Affordable Care Act and the Farm Bill. Katko pledged to continue to stand up to the president "whenever and wherever I can."

Katko went to Congress to try to make a difference by getting things done in a bipartisan fashion. Katko believed he had delivered and would be honored to continue doing that. Balter discussed her experiences listening to people's concerns throughout the district, including healthcare costs, better job opportunities, and safer communities. Balter would be a representative who listened to constituents and then goes to Washington and fights for their interests. When asked about appealing to voters turned off by politics, Balter said she spoke with lots of disengaged voters who felt like their vote did not matter. Balter emphasized every vote matters and Tuesday was an opportunity to keep elected representatives accountable. Katko understood the frustration and complacency people feel and described himself as a proven bipartisan leader, citing opioids, clean water, and economic development, as examples.

The two candidates sparred over campaign finance. Balter reiterated her pledge to not take any corporate PAC money and claimed 98 percent of her campaign contributions came from individuals. Katko said if money influenced him he would not be rated so bipartisan and suggested Balter received many individual donations from the San Francisco area, where Nancy Pelosi lives. Balter replied that Katko "really wants to run against Nancy Pelosi. Unfortunately he's not." Balter also stated that Katko took $1 million of corporate political action committee money and his voting record benefits these contributors. Katko believed Balter was being hypocritical and cited his support for a bipartisan constitutional amendment to limit money in politics, the only way Katko believed meaningful change could be achieved because of constitutional protections afforded to campaign contributions. Balter criticized the timing of Katko's support for this bill—the day before the first debate. Katko replied that Balter "can speculate all she wants," but he is "one of the most prolific legislators in all of Congress," and when he supports something, it moves.

Domestic Policy Issues

The three debates covered several other domestic policy issues, including gun violence, social welfare policy, climate change, national security, and childcare. Balter spoke about the violent attack at the Tree of Life synagogue in Pittsburgh, referencing her grandparents, who came to the United States as refugees after surviving the holocaust. "There is no place for this kind of hatred and violence in this country," Balter stated. Political leaders should condemn such attacks in no uncertain terms, particularly at the top, but President Trump has fomented divisions. Katko agreed violent attacks should be condemned and not politicized. He defended President Trump's visit to Pittsburgh as an effort to provide comfort. When asked if the Second Amendment was under attack, Katko said "no" and referenced his work as a prosecutor prosecuting gun-related crimes and sitting with parents who have lost loved ones. Katko called for a "robust" safe city task force and "robust" enforcement of existing gun laws to get illegal guns off the streets. Balter also did not think the Second Amendment was under attack, nor believed that undermining the Second Amendment was called for. Balter called for "common sense" gun safety regulations, including universal background checks, which she described as highly effective and very popular.

Katko believed this was not an issue in New York State because universal background checks are required by state law and highlighted his efforts to work with at risk children before they "get sucked up into the gang life." Balter said clarification was needed. The Concealed Carry Reciprocity Act of 2017, which Katko voted for in House, would allow people from outside of New York State, with concealed carry permits from their home state, to bring those guns into New York. Katko said in all his experience of prosecuting gun-related crimes, none involved someone who had a concealed carry permit, so this was not an issue.

In regards to social welfare policy, Katko believed Social Security and Medicare were currently solvent for several years into the future, but needed to be secured moving forward. He cited government-sponsored research into health challenges, such as Alzheimer's and cancer, and working in a bipartisan manner to collectively solve related problems. Balter said these programs helped lift millions of people out of poverty and the top 5 percent of income earners should pay in at the same rate as everyone else, which she claimed was not the case currently. Balter also claimed that Katko regularly expressed interest in lowering benefits for people entering Social Security and could not be trusted with protecting this program. Katko called this type of rhetoric "harmful" because it sought to attack and divide. Balter replied that she was laying out facts and asking for explanations on behalf of constituents.

The two candidates largely agreed on climate change. Balter highlighted how the Pentagon has identified climate disruption as one of the greatest threats to national security. Balter believed people needed to stop arguing about the science of climate change and "just address it," particularly ending America's energy dependence on fossil fuels. Renewable energy helps address climate change and provides economic development opportunities for the region by creating new "green" jobs. Katko agreed and cited his previous acknowledgment of human contributions to global warming and his support for greater funding of related scientific research. Both candidates also supported nuclear energy. Nine Mile Point is a nuclear power plant that has been in Oswego County for four decades.

The two candidates differed on the biggest threat facing the United States. Balter cited the deterioration of democracy, including attacks on a free press, an independent judiciary, America's constitutional principles, and other things that make U.S. democracy work. When asked if she had anyone in mind, Balter said she was referencing "everyone from the President on down." Katko stated Balter's response illustrated how she would not work with Republicans if elected. Katko believed terrorism was the biggest threat facing the country based on his daily briefings as a member of the Homeland Security Committee.

The candidates also differed on childcare policy. Katko introduced a paid family leave act, which was essentially "a family savings account," and wanted to create incentives for parents to go to work and incentives for employers to provide childcare benefits for working parents. Balter said many parents chose not to work because the cost of childcare would exceed income they would earn. Balter would follow Senator Kirsten Gillibrand's lead on this issue to make sure necessary support was being provided to families and to help parents join and stay in the workforce.

Local Issues
The debates included discussion of several local issues as well. Lead poisoning has been a long-term problem in Syracuse. Katko worked with federal agencies to prevent cutting lead remediation programs, increase funding, and assist with the pursuit of relevant grant funding. Balter said nationally high rates of lead poisoning in Syracuse were appalling and agreed with Katko that working with state and local officeholders to secure relevant funding was prudent. Katko echoed "being on the same page" with Balter.

Katko described the future of Interstate 81 as a "landmark issue" and worked to have Interstate 81 designated a "high priority" corridor, enabling greater access to federal funds. Katko believed the highway should run in the same general direction, citing 19 town supervisors who called for this, which would involve rebuilding in the same location or some hybrid option with a community grid. Balter supported developing a community grid because this was best for economic development, the least expensive option, had the smallest environmental impact, and would help with racial segregation created by the highway being built through the city. She believed federal funding needed to be secured and that jobs resulting from the construction should come from local companies. Balter also believed the "back and forth" on this issue had gone on way too long. New studies had resulted from interests, including the mall, who wanted to stall for another few years, as the "highway is crumbling" and economic development was needed.

Looking ahead to the next ten years, Balter expressed optimism for the future, though economic growth lagged in the district compared to other parts of the state. Infrastructure and investing in a green economy were two areas of growth that Balter was excited about pursuing in Congress. Katko believed Balter's priorities were laudable, but the root cause of the district's problems was how the state "taxes the crap out of people to death."

Notes

1. Mark Weiner, "9 issues that separate John Katko and Dana Balter in race for Congress," Syracuse.com, October 31, 2018, https://www.syracuse.com/expo/news/erry-2018/10/2676f0c50b5588/9-issues-that-separate-john-ka.html
2. Jesse Smith, "On healthcare, Faso and Delgado differ drastically," *Hudson Valley One*, October 21, 2018, https://hudsonvalleyone.com/2018/10/21/on-healthcare-faso-and-delgado-differ-drastically/
3. Nina Shutzman, "Faso talks healthcare, education, immigration," *Poughkeepsie Journal*, March 3, 2017, https://www.poughkeepsiejournal.com/story/news/2017/03/03/faso-talks-health-care-education-and-immigration/98696086/
4. Jesse Smith, "On healthcare, Faso and Delgado differ drastically," *Hudson Valley One*, October 21, 2018, https://hudsonvalleyone.com/2018/10/21/on-healthcare-faso-and-delgado-differ-drastically/
5. Jesse Smith, "On healthcare, Faso and Delgado differ drastically," *Hudson Valley One*, October 21, 2018, https://hudsonvalleyone.com/2018/10/21/on-healthcare-faso-and-delgado-differ-drastically/
6. This was quoted from *Claudia Tenney for Congress* at https://claudiaforcongress.com/issues/
7. Samantha Madison, "Fixing healthcare: 2 different approaches," *Observer Dispatch*, July 29, 2018, https://www.uticaod.com/news/20180729/fixing-health-care-2-differing-approaches
8. Samantha Madison, "Fixing healthcare: 2 different approaches," *Observer Dispatch*, July 29, 2018, https://www.uticaod.com/news/20180729/fixing-health-care-2-differing-approaches
9. Payne Horning, "NY-22 candidates spar over past healthcare vote," *WRVO*, August 9, 2018, https://www.wrvo.org/post/22nd-congressional-district-candidates-spar-over-past-health-care-vote

10. Luke Perry, "NY-22 Minute: Central New York Reps Explain Differing Their Tax Cut Votes," Utica College Center of Public Affairs and Election Research, December 21, 2017, https://www.ucpublicaffairs.com/home/2017/12/21/central-ny-house-reps-explain-their-split-tax-cut-votes-by-luke-perry
11. Luke Perry, "NY-22 Minute: Central New York Reps Explain Differing Their Tax Cut Votes," Utica College Center of Public Affairs and Election Research, December 21, 2017, https://www.ucpublicaffairs.com/home/2017/12/21/central-ny-house-reps-explain-their-split-tax-cut-votes-by-luke-perry
12. Luke Perry, "NY-22 Minute: Central New York Reps Explain Differing Their Tax Cut Votes," Utica College Center of Public Affairs and Election Research, December 21, 2017, https://www.ucpublicaffairs.com/home/2017/12/21/central-ny-house-reps-explain-their-split-tax-cut-votes-by-luke-perry
13. Luke Perry, "NY-22 Minute: Central New York Reps Explain Differing Their Tax Cut Votes," Utica College Center of Public Affairs and Election Research, December 21, 2017, https://www.ucpublicaffairs.com/home/2017/12/21/central-ny-house-reps-explain-their-split-tax-cut-votes-by-luke-perry
14. Luke Perry, "NY-22 Minute: Central New York Reps Explain Differing Their Tax Cut Votes," Utica College Center of Public Affairs and Election Research, December 21, 2017, https://www.ucpublicaffairs.com/home/2017/12/21/central-ny-house-reps-explain-their-split-tax-cut-votes-by-luke-perry
15. Jim McCllenand and Jeffrey Werling, "How the 2017 Tax Act Affects CBO's Projections," *The Congressional Budget Office,* April 20, 2018, https://www.cbo.gov/publication/53787
16. Delgado stated this during the first debate. See: https://www.c-span.org/video/?453677-1/york-22nd-congressional-district-debate
17. This was retrieved from https://delgadoforcongress.com/
18. Samantha Madison, "Tenney, Brindisi talks taxes, price increases," *Observer Dispatch,* August 26, 2018, https://www.uticaod.com/news/20180826/tenney-brindisi-talk-taxes-price-increases
19. Delgado stated this during the first debate. See: https://www.c-span.org/video/?453677-1/york-22nd-congressional-district-debate
20. Howard Gleckman, "Why the 2017 Tax Cuts are an Election-Year Bust," *Forbes,* August 29, 2018, https://www.forbes.com/sites/howardgleckman/2018/08/29/why-the-2017-tax-cuts-are-an-election-year-bust/#2f51acf92eb3

21. Howard Gleckman, "Why the 2017 Tax Cuts are an Election-Year Bust," *Forbes,* August 29, 2018, https://www.forbes.com/sites/howardgleckman/2018/08/29/why-the-2017-tax-cuts-are-an-election-year-bust/#2f51acf92eb3
22. Jordan Laird, "Vulnerable New York Republicans Resort to racial campaign ads," *City and State New York,* September 26, 2018, https://www.cityandstateny.com/articles/politics/campaigns-elections/chris-collins-racist-campaign-ads-trending.html
23. Opinion, "John Faso is Race-Baiting His Opponent," *The New York Times,* July 18, 2018, https://www.nytimes.com/2018/07/18/opinion/editorials/john-faso-antonio-delgado-congress-19th.html?rref=collection%2Fsectioncollection%2Fopinion-editorials&module=inline
24. Opinion, "Rep. John Faso Responds: Rap Music and Politics," *The New York Times,* July 20, 2018, https://www.nytimes.com/2018/07/20/opinion/john-faso.html?module=inline&login=email&auth=login-email
25. Nathanial Rackich, "25 House Districts That Could Decide the House in 2018," *Five Thirty Eight,* August 16, 2018, https://fivethirtyeight.com/features/25-districts-that-could-decide-the-house-in-2018/
26. Luke Perry, "Sockpuppet Social: NY-22, Political Ethics, and The Post Truth Era," *Stateline New York,* October 1, 2018, https://statelineny.atavist.com/sockpuppet-social?preview
27. 2016 Republican NY-22 Primary Debate at *WIBX News,* June 13, 2016, https://www.youtube.com/watch?v=1xpeqCGb834
28. Melanie Zanona, "Vulnerable Republicans embraces Trump in NY," *The Hill,* March 13, 2018, https://thehill.com/homenews/house/378037-vulnerable-republican-embraces-trump-in-ny
29. "Rep. Claudia Tenney Talks Trump, Working with Democrats, and her Re-Election Campaign," *Elected News,* June 7, 2018, https://www.youtube.com/watch?v=Q8131kTP0Ds&t=321s
30. Michael Grynbaum, "Trump Calls the New Media The 'Enemy of the American People,'" *The New York Times,* February 17, 2017, https://www.nytimes.com/2017/02/17/business/trump-calls-the-news-media-the-enemy-of-the-people.html
31. Luke Perry, "NY-22 Minute: Tenney's Social Media Series Criticizes News Media," The Utica College Center of Public Affairs and Election Research, July 2, 2018, https://www.ucpublicaffairs.com/home/2018/6/30/b3cmquc0djn62uo28gptwrrkgqf8zs
32. Full disclosure: I have served as an unpaid political analyst and columnist for the paper since in 2016.
33. "Rep. Claudia Tenney Talks Trump, Working with Democrats, and her Re-Election Campaign," *Elected News,* June 7, 2018, https://www.youtube.com/watch?v=Q8131kTP0Ds&t=321s

34. For example, see "Tenney: Bill would help promote non-opioid pain treatment," *Observer Dispatch*, May 15, 2018, http://www.uticaod.com/news/20180515/tenney-bill-would-help-promote-non-opioid-pain-treatment
35. Greg Mason, "Q & A with Claudia Tenney; Health care, media & more," *Observer Dispatch*, January 2, 2018, https://www.uticaod.com/news/20180102/qampa-with-claudia-tenney-health-care-media-and-more
36. Greg Mason, "Q & A with Claudia Tenney; Health care, media & more," *Observer Dispatch*, January 2, 2018, https://www.uticaod.com/news/20180102/qampa-with-claudia-tenney-health-care-media-and-more
37. Jeffrey Gottfriend and Michael Barthel, "Almost seven-in-ten Americans have news fatigue, more among Republicans," *Pew Research Center*, June 5, 2018, http://www.pewresearch.org/fact-tank/2018/06/05/almost-seven-in-ten-americans-have-news-fatigue-more-among-republicans/
38. Michael Barthel and Amy Mitchell, "Americans' Attitudes About the News Media Deeply Divided Along Partisan Lines," *Pew Research Center*, May 10, 2017, http://www.journalism.org/2017/05/10/americans-attitudes-about-the-news-media-deeply-divided-along-partisan-lines/
39. Nicole Gaudiano, "Tenney highlights 'notorious' background of Brindisi's father," *USA Today*, July 14, 2017, https://www.pressconnects.com/story/news/2017/07/14/tenney-highlights-notorious-background-brindisis-father/479172001/
40. Nicole Gaudiano, "Tenney highlights 'notorious' background of Brindisi's father," *USA Today*, July 14, 2017, https://www.pressconnects.com/story/news/2017/07/14/tenney-highlights-notorious-background-brindisis-father/479172001/
41. Nicole Gaudiano, "Tenney highlights 'notorious' background of Brindisi's father," *USA Today*, July 14, 2017, https://www.pressconnects.com/story/news/2017/07/14/tenney-highlights-notorious-background-brindisis-father/479172001/
42. Nicole Gaudiano, "Tenney highlights 'notorious' background of Brindisi's father," *USA Today*, July 14, 2017, https://www.pressconnects.com/story/news/2017/07/14/tenney-highlights-notorious-background-brindisis-father/479172001/
43. Marisa Schultz, "GOP Congresswomen call Dem opponent's family 'thuggish' criminals," *The New York Post*, September 18, 2018, https://nypost.com/2018/09/18/gop-congressman-calls-dem-opponents-family-thuggish-criminals/
44. Marisa Schultz, "GOP Congresswomen call Dem opponent's family 'thuggish' criminals," *The New York Post*, September 18, 2018, https://nypost.

com/2018/09/18/gop-congressman-calls-dem-opponents-family-thuggish-criminals/
45. Rocco LaDuca, "The Mob Files Day 7: How it all Ended," *The Observer Dispatch,* May 9, 2009, https://www.uticaod.com/x1518870796/The-Mob-Files-Day-7
46. Rocco LaDuca, "Man says city employee hit him, gas line with vehicle," *The Observer Dispatch,* April 4, 2014, https://www.uticaod.com/article/20140404/News/140409525
47. Luke Austin, "Trial Date Set for Utica City Worker Andrew Brindisi," *WIBX News,* September 30, 2014, http://wibx950.com/trial-date-set-for-utica-city-worker-andrew-brindisi/
48. Luke Austin, "Utica City Worker Gets Probation for March Hit-and-Run Accident," *WIBX News,* December 17, 2014, http://wibx950.com/utica-city-worker-gets-probation-for-march-hit-and-run-accident/
49. Marisa Schultz, "GOP Congresswomen call Dem opponent's family "thuggish" criminals," *The New York Post,* September 18, 2018, https://nypost.com/2018/09/18/gop-congressman-calls-dem-opponents-family-thuggish-criminals/
50. "Latest Tenney Attack Another Cheap Shot," *Observer Dispatch*, September 21, 2018, https://www.uticaod.com/opinion/20180921/our-view-latest-tenney-attack-another-cheap-shot
51. "Latest Tenney Attack Another Cheap Shot," *Observer Dispatch*, September 21, 2018, https://www.uticaod.com/opinion/20180921/our-view-latest-tenney-attack-another-cheap-shot
52. "Latest Tenney Attack Another Cheap Shot," *Observer Dispatch*, September 21, 2018, https://www.uticaod.com/opinion/20180921/our-view-latest-tenney-attack-another-cheap-shot
53. Mark Weiner, "Fact Check: Is John Katko's ad about Dana Balter's taxes accurate?" *Syracuse.com*, October 11, 2018, https://www.syracuse.com/politics/index.ssf/2018/10/fact_check_is_john_katkos_ad_about_dana_balters_taxes_accurate.html
54. Robert Harding, "Katko: Balter misleading voters about ties to New York," *The Citizen*, August 16, 2018, https://auburnpub.com/blogs/eye_on_ny/katko-balter-misleading-voters-about-ties-to-central-new-york/article_1e03b25e-d0b8-11e8-83ae-bf180f73fbe9.html
55. Robert Harding, "Katko: Balter misleading voters about ties to New York," *The Citizen*, August 16, 2018, https://auburnpub.com/blogs/eye_on_ny/katko-balter-misleading-voters-about-ties-to-central-new-york/article_1e03b25e-d0b8-11e8-83ae-bf180f73fbe9.html
56. Matthew Hamilton, "Who's a carpetbagger?" *Times Union*, September 19, 2016, https://www.timesunion.com/tuplus-local/article/Who-s-a-carpetbagger-9233205.php

57. "Katko fires back at claim that campaign contributions influenced a vote," *Syracuse.com*, October 25, 2018, https://www.localsyr.com/election/your-local-election/katko-fires-back-at-balter-s-claim-that-campaign-contributions-influenced-a-vote/1549873355
58. "Katko fires back at claim that campaign contributions influenced a vote," *Syracuse.com*, October 25, 2018, https://www.localsyr.com/election/your-local-election/katko-fires-back-at-balter-s-claim-that-campaign-contributions-influenced-a-vote/1549873355
59. Full audio of the debate was retrieved at https://www.wamc.org/post/listen-or-watch-ny-19-debate
60. There is no audio or video of the forum. I was covered the event as a journalist.
61. Full video of the debate was obtained at: https://www.c-span.org/video/?453677-1/york-22nd-congressional-district-debate
62. Video of the debate was accessed at https://www.youtube.com/watch?v=yS68ZDSI6oQ
63. Video of the debate was accessed at https://cnycentral.com/news/local/watch-full-cnycentral-congressional-debate-between-katko-balter
64. Video of the debate was accessed at https://www.youtube.com/watch?v=Ce5w4hBY5Ok
65. These questions were asked during a speed round, so detailed explanations were not provided.

CHAPTER 3

Polling

Abstract This chapter examines polling conducted during the 2018 campaigns in NY-19, NY-22, and NY-24.

Keywords Donald Trump • 2018 Midterm election • Siena Research Institute • Zogby Analytics • NY-19 • NY-22 • NY-24 • John Katko • Anthony Brindisi • Antonio Delgado

Accurate, independent polling of local races is a persistent challenge in U.S. politics. Educational institutions played a vital role providing reliable polling of House campaigns in Central New York, particularly the Siena College Research Institute. There were three polls conducted in NY-19 during the 2018 campaign, two by the Siena College Research Institute and one by Monmouth University. Polling occurred in consecutive months between August and November of 2018. Each found both candidates within the margin of error. John Faso posted his biggest lead of five points in August. The race tightened in the closing months as Faso's favorability declined and undecided voters broke toward Delgado, erasing Faso's advantage.

Siena College August NY-19 Poll

Likely voters in NY-19 favored John Faso over Antonio Delgado 45 percent to 40 percent (4.8 margin of error) in August of 2018. Thirteen percent were undecided.[1] Both parties exhibited widespread support for their respective candidates. Eighty-one percent of Democrats supported Delgado, while 76 percent of Republicans supported Faso. Fifteen percent of Republicans and 18 percent of independents were undecided. Faso had a six-point advantage with independents. Faso led men by over 20 points and received strong support in the Northern half of district. Delgado was ahead with women by nearly 10 points and received strong support in the Southeastern portion of the district, particularly Ulster and Dutchess counties (Tables 3.1 and 3.2).

Though ahead, Faso was not particularly well liked. Voters were nearly evenly divided about his favorability. In contrast, Delgado was viewed

Table 3.1 August NY-19 poll: candidate support

	John Faso	*Anthony Delgado*	*Don't know/other*
Total	45%	40%	13%
Democrats	13%	81%	6%
Republicans	76%	8%	15%
Independents	44%	38%	18%

Source: "Faso leads Delgado by 5 points, 45–40," Siena College Research Institute, August 30, 2018, https://scri.siena.edu/2018/08/30/faso-leads-delgado-by-5-points-45-40-percent/

Table 3.2 August NY-19 poll: gender and geography

	John Faso	*Anthony Delgado*	*Don't know/other*
Men	53%	32%	14%
Women	38%	47%	16%
Dutchess and Ulster counties	36%	49%	14%
Broome, Delaware, Otsego, and Sullivan counties	51%	28%	21%
Columbia, Greene, Montgomery, Rensselaer, and Schoharie counties	53%	36%	11%

Source: "Faso leads Delgado by 5 points, 45–40," Siena College Research Institute, August 30, 2018, https://scri.siena.edu/2018/08/30/faso-leads-delgado-by-5-points-45-40-percent/

much more favorably than unfavorably, though over 40 percent had no opinion or didn't know. Lack of opinion was less pronounced for Faso, at 25 percent, but this was still high for an incumbent who held office for nearly two years. If messaging is working, constituents should be familiar enough with an incumbent's body of work to form an opinion. Indicators of national political attitudes were not ideal, nor awful, for Faso. A plurality of constituents wanted Republicans to maintain control of the House of Representatives, five points higher than who prefer Democratic control. President Trump's approval rating was on par with national attitudes, 45 percent, though slightly more constituents viewed him unfavorably (Tables 3.3, 3.4, and 3.5).

Table 3.3 August NY-19 poll: favorability of candidates

	Anthony Delgado				*John Faso*			
	Total	Dem.	Rep.	Ind.	Total	Dem.	Rep.	Ind.
Favorable	34	65	12	30	37	15	59	32
Unfavorable	22	11	32	25	38	72	14	36
Don't care or no opinion	44	24	56	45	24	13	27	32

Source: "Faso leads Delgado by 5 points, 45–40," Siena College Research Institute, August 30, 2018, https://scri.siena.edu/2018/08/30/faso-leads-delgado-by-5-points-45-40-percent/

Table 3.4 August NY-19 poll: presidential approval rating

	Total	Democrats	Republicans	Ind./other
Approve	45%	10%	75%	49%
Disapprove	47%	85%	17%	44%
Don't know or no opinion	8%	5%	8%	7%

		Delgado supporters		*Faso supporters*
Approve		7%		79%
Disapprove		90%		15%
Don't know or no opinion		3%		6%

Source: "Faso leads Delgado by 5 points, 45–40," Siena College Research Institute, August 30, 2018, https://scri.siena.edu/2018/08/30/faso-leads-delgado-by-5-points-45-40-percent/

Table 3.5 August NY-19 poll: party control of house

	Total	Democrat	Republican	Ind./other
Democrat	43%	86%	8%	39%
Republican	48%	10%	87%	45%
Don't know or no opinion	9%	5%	5%	16%

	Delgado supporters	Faso supporters
Democrat	89%	8%
Republican	8%	89%
Don't know or no opinion	4%	3%

Source: "Faso leads Delgado by 5 points, 45–40," Siena College Research Institute, August 30, 2018, https://scri.siena.edu/2018/08/30/faso-leads-delgado-by-5-points-45-40-percent/

MONMOUTH UNIVERSITY SEPTEMBER NY-19 POLL

Monmouth University polled NY-19 in September of 2018. Delgado led Faso by two points, 45 percent to 43 percent, among potential voters (4.9-point margin of error).[2] Respondents were very interested in the NY-19 election, though just one in five were following the race closely. President Trump was viewed slightly more favorably than in the earlier Siena poll, but constituents who strongly disapproved of the president was eight points higher than those who strongly approved.

Trump was clearly a central consideration as voters prepared to go to the polls. Nearly 70 percent of voters said it was "very important" for them to cast their Congressional vote to support/oppose President Trump. A plurality of respondents (32 percent) thought Faso had exhibited the "right amount of support" for President Trump, while a similar margin (29 percent) believed he was too supportive of the president.

Like the Siena poll, the Monmouth poll found a preference for Republican control of the House, though the level of support was slightly smaller. At the same time, the number of constituents who didn't know, or had opinion, doubled from 9 percent in Siena poll to 20 percent in the Monmouth poll. A plurality were unsure if Delgado would be too supportive of Nancy Pelosi if elected. More respondents thought he would provide the "right amount of support" (30 percent) than be "too supportive" (21 percent).

Healthcare (29 percent) was identified as the most important issue in deciding how to vote, followed by immigration (20 percent) and gun control (15 percent). Respondents were evenly divided over the Tax Cuts and Job Act, though people more strongly disapproved than strongly approved (Tables 3.6, 3.7, 3.8, 3.9, and 3.10).

Table 3.6 Monmouth NY-19 poll: candidate support

	Anthony Delgado	John Faso
Who respondents will vote for	45%	43%
Favorable	36%	34%
Unfavorable	21%	33%

Source: "New York: Voters Divided in CD19," Monmouth University Poll, September 12, 2018, https://www.monmouth.edu/polling-institute/documents/monmouthpoll_ny_091218.pdf/

Table 3.7 Monmouth NY-19 poll: interest in house election

A lot	60%
A little	26%
Not at all	14%
Don't know	0%

Source: "New York: Voters Divided in CD19," Monmouth University Poll, September 12, 2018, https://www.monmouth.edu/polling-institute/documents/monmouthpoll_ny_091218.pdf/

Table 3.8 Monmouth NY-19 poll: President Trump's approval rating

Strongly approve	35%
Somewhat approve	13%
Somewhat disapprove	4%
Strongly disapprove	43%

Source: "New York: Voters Divided in CD19," Monmouth University Poll, September 12, 2018, https://www.monmouth.edu/polling-institute/documents/monmouthpoll_ny_091218.pdf/

Table 3.9 Monmouth NY-19 poll: party control of house

Republicans	39%
Democrats	37%
Doesn't matter	20%
Don't know	4%

Source: "New York: Voters Divided in CD19," Monmouth University Poll, September 12, 2018, https://www.monmouth.edu/polling-institute/documents/monmouthpoll_ny_091218.pdf/

Table 3.10 Monmouth NY-19 poll: important issues

Healthcare	29%
Immigration	20%
Gun control	15%
Taxes	11%
Job creation	10%

Source: "New York: Voters Divided in CD19," Monmouth University Poll, September 12, 2018, https://www.monmouth.edu/polling-institute/documents/monmouthpoll_ny_091218.pdf/

SIENA COLLEGE OCTOBER NY-19 POLL

Faso and Delgado were virtually tied on the eve of the election. Faso held a narrow single-point lead (4.6 margin of error), but his five-point lead in August had collapsed.[3] Undecided voters fell from 13 percent to 7 percent, and broke in Faso's direction, but Delgado gained five points among women. These gains correlated with growing support for Delgado throughout the district, as he expanded his lead among his geographic base, Dutchess and Ulster counties, while closing gaps elsewhere. Faso lost majority support in the other two geographic blocks polled (Broome, Delaware, Otsego, and Sullivan counties) and (Columbia, Greene, Montgomery, Rensselaer, and Schoharie counties). Favorability was another advantage for Delgado. Voters had increasingly developed attitudes toward candidate favorability, and the net effect was positive for Delgado. Delgado remained slightly more favorable than unfavorable, while Faso fell five points underwater, as he lost ground with both Republicans and Democrats.

Attitudes toward President Trump were relatively stable between August and October. Likely NY-19 voters remained slightly more disapproving than approving. There was a significant change among independents. Trump went from a plus five-point approval rating to minus 1. Voters continued to prefer Republican support of the House, though by a slightly smaller margin. Democrats became more supportive of Democratic control, while Republicans became more supportive of Republican control. This was another area where a major shift among independents was evident. In August, independents went from preferring Republican control by six points to Democratic control by two points (Tables 3.11, 3.12, 3.13, 3.14, and 3.15).

Table 3.11 Siena NY-19 poll: candidate support

	John Faso	Anthony Delgado	Don't know/other
Total	44%	43%	13%
Democrats	12%	79%	6%
Republicans	71%	13%	16%
Independents	43%	42%	15%

Source: "Separated By 1 Point: Faso 44%; Delgado 43%; Others 6%; Undecided 7%," Siena College Research Institute, October 22, 2018, https://scri.siena.edu/2018/10/22/new-york-19-oct-2018/

Table 3.12 Siena NY-19 poll: gender and geography

	John Faso	Anthony Delgado	Don't know/other
Men	53%	34%	12%
Women	35%	52%	13%
Dutchess and Ulster counties	45%	47%	9%
Broome, Delaware, Otsego, and Sullivan counties	41%	43%	16%
Columbia, Greene, Montgomery, Rensselaer, and Schoharie counties	44%	40%	17%

Source: "Separated By 1 Point: Faso 44%; Delgado 43%; Others 6%; Undecided 7%," Siena College Research Institute, October 22, 2018, https://scri.siena.edu/2018/10/22/new-york-19-oct-2018/

Table 3.13 Siena NY-19 poll: favorability of candidates

	Anthony Delgado				John Faso			
	Total	Dem.	Rep.	Ind.	Total	Dem.	Rep.	Ind.
Favorable	42%	72%	20%	36%	40%	12%	63%	41%
Unfavorable	41%	15%	63%	40%	46%	77%	20%	45%
Don't care or no opinion	18%	13%	17%	24%	14%	11%	16%	14%

Source: "Separated By 1 Point: Faso 44%; Delgado 43%; Others 6%; Undecided 7%," Siena College Research Institute, October 22, 2018, https://scri.siena.edu/2018/10/22/new-york-19-oct-2018/

Table 3.14 Siena NY-19 poll: presidential approval rating

	Total	Democrats	Republicans	Ind./other
Approve	46%	13%	73%	46%
Disapprove	49%	86%	18%	47%
Don't know or no opinion	6%	2%	9%	6%

	Delgado supporters	Faso supporters
Approve	4%	89%
Disapprove	93%	6%
Don't know or no opinion	3%	5%

Source: "Separated By 1 Point: Faso 44%; Delgado 43%; Others 6%; Undecided 7%," Siena College Research Institute, October 22, 2018, https://scri.siena.edu/2018/10/22/new-york-19-oct-2018/

Table 3.15 Siena NY-19 poll: party control of house

	Total	Democrat	Republican	Ind./other
Democrat	45%	82%	13%	46%
Republican	48%	13%	81%	44%
Don't know or no opinion	7%	5%	6%	10%

	Delgado supporters	Faso supporters
Democrat	93%	2%
Republican	3%	94%
Don't know or no opinion	4%	4%

Source: "Separated By 1 Point: Faso 44%; Delgado 43%; Others 6%; Undecided 7%," Siena College Research Institute, October 22, 2018, https://scri.siena.edu/2018/10/22/new-york-19-oct-2018/

ZOGBY ANALYTICS NY-22 POLL (MAY 2018)

Three independent polls were conducted in NY-22, two by the Siena College Research Institute and one by Zogby Analytics. Anthony Brindisi led in every poll and was consistently viewed more favorably than Claudia Tenney. Brindisi initially faced low name recognition, which he was able to improve over time. Tenney faced diminished support among Republicans, and her inability to bring fellow party members back into the fold by Election Day negatively impacted her prospects for reelection.

The first independent poll for the race was conducted by Zogby Analytics in May of 2018, the earliest polling of the three races examined here.[4] Anthony Brindisi was ahead among likely NY-22 voters by seven points (5.2-point margin of error). Thirteen percent were undecided. Among the undecided, 55 percent preferred Brindisi, while 45 percent preferred Tenney. Brindisi had strong support among Democrats, while Tenney had just 71 percent support among Republicans, 29 percent of whom supported Brindisi.

The Zogby poll pointed to other clear advantages for Brindisi. Brindisi was up 56 percent to 44 percent in Oneida County, where nearly 60 percent of likely voters viewed him favorably. Brindisi also received strong support from women (59 percent) and independents (57 percent). Just 41 percent of likely voters viewed Tenney favorably compared to 52 percent who viewed her unfavorably. Thirty-seven percent viewed Tenney "very unfavorably." Brindisi was above water in favorability (plus 13 points) but nearly half of respondents were unfamiliar enough with him to judge (Table 3.16).

Table 3.16 Zogby analytics poll

	Anthony Brindisi	*Claudia Tenney*
Likely NY-22 voters	47	40
Undecided NY-22 voters	55	45
Oneida County	56	44
Democrats	90	10
Republicans	71	29
Women	59	41
Independents	57	43

Source: "Anthony Brindisi holds a double-digit lead over Claudia Tenney for the NY 22nd Congressional seat," Zogby Poll, May 2, 2018, https://zogbyanalytics.com/news/844-the-zogby-poll-anthony-brindisi-holds-a-double-digit-lead-over-claudia-tenney-for-the-ny-22nd-congressional-seat-the-race-could-signal-dems-winning-back-the-house-of-representatives-millennials-women-and-independents-supporting-brindisi-over-tenney

Siena College Research Institute August NY-22 Poll

The Siena poll four months later exhibited parallels and differences with the Zogby poll.[5] The biggest difference was the margin of Brindisi's lead, which Siena had at two points (5.2-point margin of error).[6] Brindisi was much less supported among independents. Tenney's support among Republicans was similarly low (66 percent) and she was viewed more unfavorably than favorably. This was much lower than Brindisi, who was plus 17 in favorability.

Though Tenney was not popular, a majority of likely voters in NY-22 wanted Republicans to maintain House control. Just 40 percent preferred Democratic control. Independents favored Republican control by 11 points, while splitting support between both candidates. Thirteen percent of Brindisi supporters favored Republican control.

These numbers suggest a portion of the electorate separated their party attitudes from their attitudes toward the two candidates. In particular, some Republicans and independents were willing to support Brindisi even if their political ideology was more conservative than his. Conversely, the Republican Party label was not so much a problem for Claudia Tenney as people's perceptions of her.

Siena found President Trump was still popular in NY-22. Fifty-one percent of NY-22 likely voters approved of his job performance, compared to 44 percent who did not. This was five points lower than his NY-22 vote share in 2016, but still a majority, and still higher than Tenney's approval rating. Trump's favorability was also much higher in the district than statewide and nationally. Even upstate, which is more Republican, most voters viewed Trump unfavorably.[7] This created a challenge for Brindisi. His approach was to sparingly mention the president, typically in times of strong agreement or disapproval. Areas of agreement typically pertained to certain positions Trump stated on the 2016 campaign trail, including his proposed infrastructure bill or his support for Medicare being able to negotatie drug prices, not his actions as president. This tactically enabled Brindisi to demonstrate alignment with Trump, while contrasting himself with two years of unified Republican government (Tables 3.17, 3.18, 3.19, 3.20, and 3.21).

Table 3.17 Siena NY-22 poll: candidate support

	Anthony Brindisi	Claudia Tenney	Don't know/other
Total	46%	44%	10%
Democrats	80%	14%	6%
Republicans	24%	66%	12%
Independents	44%	43%	8%

Source: "Incumbent Tenney and Challenger Brindisi Locked in Dead Heat," Siena College Research Institute, August 29, 2018, https://scri.siena.edu/2018/08/29/incumbent-tenney-challenger-brindisi-locked-in-a-near-dead-heat/

Table 3.18 Siena NY-22 poll: favorability of candidates

	Anthony Brindisi				Claudia Tenney			
	Total	Dem.	Rep.	Ind.	Total	Dem.	Rep.	Ind.
Favorable	44%	64%	31%	44%	42%	15%	60%	44%
Unfavorable	27%	13%	37%	28%	47%	77%	28%	47%
Don't care or no opinion	29%	23%	32%	29%	11%	8%	12%	10%

Source: "Incumbent Tenney and Challenger Brindisi Locked in Dead Heat," Siena College Research Institute, August 29, 2018, https://scri.siena.edu/2018/08/29/incumbent-tenney-challenger-brindisi-locked-in-a-near-dead-heat/

Table 3.19 Siena NY-22 poll: gender and geography

	Anthony Brindisi	Claudia Tenney	Don't know/other
Men	38%	51%	7%
Women	54%	38%	11%
Broome/Tioga	46%	42%	12%
Chenango/Cortland/Madison	49%	45%	7%
Herkimer/Oneida/Oswego	44%	46%	10%

Source: "Incumbent Tenney and Challenger Brindisi Locked in Dead Heat," Siena College Research Institute, August 29, 2018, https://scri.siena.edu/2018/08/29/incumbent-tenney-challenger-brindisi-locked-in-a-near-dead-heat/

Table 3.20 Siena NY-22 poll: party control of house

	Total	Democrat	Republican	Ind./other
Democrat	40%	80%	14%	38%
Republican	53%	13%	83%	49%
Don't know or no opinion	7%	7%	4%	13%

	Brindisi supporters	Tenney supporters
Democrat	80%	3%
Republican	13%	94%
Don't know or no opinion	7%	2%

Source: "Incumbent Tenney and Challenger Brindisi Locked in Dead Heat," Siena College Research Institute, August 29, 2018, https://scri.siena.edu/2018/08/29/incumbent-tenney-challenger-brindisi-locked-in-a-near-dead-heat/

Table 3.21 Siena NY-22 poll: presidential approval rating

	Total	Democrats	Republicans	Ind./other
Approve	51%	19%	73%	49%
Disapprove	44%	78%	21%	47%
Don't know or no opinion	5%	3%	6%	4%

	Brindisi supporters	Tenney supporters
Approve	15%	86%
Disapprove	83%	9%
Don't know or no opinion	2%	5%

Source: "Incumbent Tenney and Challenger Brindisi Locked in Dead Heat," Siena College Research Institute, August 29, 2018, https://scri.siena.edu/2018/08/29/incumbent-tenney-challenger-brindisi-locked-in-a-near-dead-heat/

Siena College Research Institute October NY-22 Poll

Brindisi retained a narrow one-point lead over Tenney in the October Siena Poll, though the two candidates were virtually tied.[8] Tenney was unable to erode Brindisi's standing among Republicans. Nearly one in four continued to support Brindisi over Tenney. Tenney was also unable to improve her favorability levels. Remarkably, she remained identically underwater by five points with a 42 percent favorability rating. Brindisi's unfavorability rose ten points, mostly among Republicans, but he was still plus nine points overall, and his level of support from Republicans actually rose one point.

Brindisi made significant gains among independents, receiving majority support and growing a 16-point lead over Tenney. This occurred without major shifts in Brindisi's favorability among the group, which remained constant at plus 16 points. Independents shifted in favor of Democratic House control and away from approval of President Trump. This was a bad omen for Tenney. High progressive enthusiasm, coupled with independent support and crossover Republicans, could overcome Republican's sizeable registered voter advantage in the district (Tables 3.22, 3.23, 3.24, 3.25, and 3.26).

Table 3.22 Siena NY-22 poll: candidate support

	Anthony Brindisi	Claudia Tenney	Don't know/other
Total	46%	45%	9%
Democrats	77%	17%	6%
Republicans	23%	65%	9%
Independents	54%	38%	14%

Source: "New York 22: Brindisi 46%- Tenney 45%-Undecided 9%," *Siena Research Institute*, October 24, 2018, https://scri.siena.edu/2018/10/24/new-york-22-brindisi-46-tenney-45-undecided-9/

Table 3.23 Siena NY-22 poll: favorability of candidates

	Anthony Brindisi				Claudia Tenney			
	Total	Dem.	Rep.	Ind.	Total	Dem.	Rep.	Ind.
Favorable	46%	73%	29%	48%	42%	19%	59%	34%
Unfavorable	37%	17%	52%	32%	47%	73%	29%	52%
Don't care or no opinion	16%	11%	19%	19%	11%	8%	12%	14%

Source: "New York 22: Brindisi 46%- Tenney 45%-Undecided 9%," *Siena Research Institute*, October 24, 2018, https://scri.siena.edu/2018/10/24/new-york-22-brindisi-46-tenney-45-undecided-9/

Table 3.24 Siena NY-22 poll: gender and geography

	Anthony Brindisi	Claudia Tenney	Don't know/other
Men	41%	52%	11%
Women	51%	38%	9%
Broome/Tioga	48%	44%	8%
Chenango/Cortland/Madison	47%	40%	14%
Herkimer/Oneida/Oswego	44%	49%	7%

Source: "New York 22: Brindisi 46%- Tenney 45%-Undecided 9%," *Siena Research Institute*, October 24, 2018, https://scri.siena.edu/2018/10/24/new-york-22-brindisi-46-tenney-45-undecided-9/

Table 3.25 Siena NY-22 poll: party control of house

	Total	Democrat	Republican	Ind./other
Democrat	40%	73%	17%	48%
Republican	53%	20%	76%	45%
Don't know or no opinion	7%	7%	7%	7%

	Brindisi supporters	Tenney supporters
Democrat	82%	2%
Republican	11%	95%
Don't know or no opinion	7%	2%

Source: "New York 22: Brindisi 46%- Tenney 45%-Undecided 9%," *Siena Research Institute*, October 24, 2018, https://scri.siena.edu/2018/10/24/new-york-22-brindisi-46-tenney-45-undecided-9/

Table 3.26 Siena NY-22 poll: presidential approval rating

	Total	Democrats	Republicans	Ind./other
Approve	53%	27%	71%	46%
Disapprove	43%	70%	25%	49%
Don't know or no opinion	5%	3%	4%	5%

	Brindisi supporters	Tenney supporters
Approve	15%	91%
Disapprove	82%	7%
Don't know or no opinion	3%	2%

Source: "New York 22: Brindisi 46%- Tenney 45%-Undecided 9%," *Siena Research Institute*, October 24, 2018, https://scri.siena.edu/2018/10/24/new-york-22-brindisi-46-tenney-45-undecided-9/

SIENA COLLEGE RESEARCH INSTITUTE AUGUST NY-24 POLL

Two independent polls were conducted in NY-24, both by the Siena College Research Institute. John Katko had a comfortable lead of 15 points and majority support in each. This was lower than his election margin in 2014 and reelection margin in 2016, but still a much stronger position than his Republican colleagues Claudia Tenney and John Faso.

The first Siena poll of likely NY-24 voters was conducted in August of 2018.[9] Katko had a 15-point lead (4.8 margin of error), 54–39 percent. Katko received strong support from Republicans and held an 11-point lead among independents. Balter's Democratic support (72 percent) was lower than one might expect, considering she ran farther to the left than Delgado or Brindisi. Balter also trailed Katko by double digits with independents, a crucial component to Katko's prospects of retaining the seat. Balter's geographic base was Syracuse, where she had a 32-point advantage over Katko. Katko dominated the remainder of the district, up 14 points in the rest of Onondaga County and 35 points in a combination of Cayuga, Oswego, and Wayne counties.

In contrast to Faso and Tenney, Katko was viewed favorably by a majority of voters with a plus 17 favorability rating. Katko's favorability was also much higher than Balter's. Balter was nine points above water; however, 45 percent were unsure, suggesting lack of name recognition. All three Republican incumbents did well among men, though Katko did the best, with a 31 percent advantage over Balter. Women were evenly divided in NY-24. This was a bit surprising because NY-24 is a Democratic district and liberal women, particularly grassroots organizers, were a significant political force this election cycle. For instance, Anthony Brindisi had a 16-point advantage among women at the same point in time. Voters preferred Republican House control in line with the other two districts examined here. The margin was narrow, more like NY-19, than NY-22. The president had a 45 percent approval rating, also similar to NY-19, and was four points under water (Tables 3.27, 3.28, 3.29, 3.30, and 3.31).

Table 3.27 Siena NY-24 poll: candidate support

	John Katko	Dana Balter	Don't know/other
Total	54%	39%	8%
Democrats	21%	72%	8%
Republicans	86%	9%	5%
Independent	51%	40%	10%

Source: "Katko has 15 point Lead Over Balter, 54–39 percent," Siena College Research Institute, August 30, 2018, https://scri.siena.edu/2018/08/27/katko-has-15-point-lead-over-balter-54-39-percent/

Table 3.28 Siena NY-24 poll: geography and gender

	John Katko	Dana Balter	Don't know/other
Syracuse	30%	62%	7%
Rest of Onondaga County	53%	39%	8%
Cayuga, Oswego, and Wayne counties	65%	30%	6%
Men	63%	32%	5%
Women	45%	45%	9%

Source: "Katko has 15 point Lead Over Balter, 54–39 percent," Siena College Research Institute, August 30, 2018, https://scri.siena.edu/2018/08/27/katko-has-15-point-lead-over-balter-54-39-percent/

Table 3.29 Siena NY-24 poll: favorability of candidates

	John Katko				Dana Balter			
	Total	Dem.	Rep.	Ind.	Total	Dem.	Rep.	Ind.
Favorable	53%	30%	76%	49%	32%	58%	7%	36%
Unfavorable	36%	61%	10%	40%	23%	12%	37%	20%
Don't care or no opinion	11%	9%	13%	10%	45%	31%	57%	43%

Source: "Katko has 15 point Lead Over Balter, 54–39 percent," Siena College Research Institute, August 30, 2018, https://scri.siena.edu/2018/08/27/katko-has-15-point-lead-over-balter-54-39-percent/

Table 3.30 Siena NY-24 poll: party control of house

	Total	Democrat	Republican	Ind./other
Democrat	45%	84%	7%	52%
Republican	47%	10%	88%	37%
Don't know or no opinion	8%	6%	5%	11%

	Balter supporters	Katko supporters
Democrat	89%	13%
Republican	5%	79%
Don't know or no opinion	6%	8%

Source: "Katko has 15 point Lead Over Balter, 54–39 percent," Siena College Research Institute, August 30, 2018, https://scri.siena.edu/2018/08/27/katko-has-15-point-lead-over-balter-54-39-percent/

Table 3.31 Siena NY-24 poll: presidential approval rating

	Total	Democrats	Republicans	Ind./other
Approve	45%	10%	80%	39%
Disapprove	49%	82%	15%	58%
Don't know or no opinion	6%	8%	4%	3%

	Balter supporters	Katko supporters
Approve	7%	73%
Disapprove	89%	21%
Don't know or no opinion	4%	6%

Source: "Katko has 15 point Lead Over Balter, 54–39 percent," Siena College Research Institute, August 30, 2018, https://scri.siena.edu/2018/08/27/katko-has-15-point-lead-over-balter-54-39-percent/

SIENA COLLEGE RESEARCH INSTITUTE OCTOBER POLL

The Siena poll conducted in October of 2018 found Katko's lead of 15 points virtually unchanged from August, 53 percent–39 percent.[10] Katko also retained a 15-point favorability advantage over Balter though his favorability among Democrats dropped 12 points between August and October. Meanwhile, Balter's favorability flipped. Twenty percent more voters developed an opinion of her, suggesting enhanced name recognition, but Balter's favorability went from plus 9 to minus 12 points. Among independents, Balter similarly flipped from up 16 to minus 12 points. One in four voters still had no opinion, including one in three Republicans.

The president became a little more popular as voters were evenly divided over approval and disapproval, 48 percent for each. Trump lost a little ground among Republicans, but gained some with Democrats. He rose from 39/58 approval with independents to 48/47. Balter supporters overwhelmingly disapproved of Trump, while Katko supporters overwhelmingly approved. The latter was an interesting dynamic, considering Katko went to great lengths to publicly distance himself from the president. This data suggests that doing so did not negatively impact him among Trump supporters. Preference for House control was relatively unchanged overall, but independents shifted significantly. In August, independents preferred Democratic control by 15 points. By October, this margin had been replaced with an even split (Tables 3.32, 3.33, 3.34, 3.35, and 3.36).

Table 3.32 Siena NY-24 poll: candidate support

	John Katko	Dana Balter
Total	53%	39%
Democrats	20%	72%
Republicans	82%	10%
Independent/other	53%	40%

Source: "Katko Maintains Double-Digit Lead Over Balter." Siena College Research Institute, October 28, 2018, https://scri.siena.edu/2018/10/28/katko-maintains-double-digit-lead-over-balter/

Table 3.33 Siena NY-24 poll: geography and gender

	John Katko	Dana Balter	Don't know/other
Syracuse	26%	64%	10%
Rest of Onondaga County	55%	36%	8%
Cayuga, Oswego, and Wayne counties	60%	34%	6%
Men	62%	30%	9%
Women	46%	48%	7%

Source: "Katko Maintains Double-Digit Lead Over Balter." Siena College Research Institute, October 28, 2018, https://scri.siena.edu/2018/10/28/katko-maintains-double-digit-lead-over-balter/

Table 3.34 Siena NY-24 poll: favorability of candidates

	John Katko				Dana Balter			
	Total	Dem.	Rep.	Ind.	Total	Dem.	Rep.	Ind.
Favorable	48%	18%	76%	46%	33%	60%	10%	34%
Unfavorable	39%	68%	13%	43%	42%	21%	57%	46%
Don't care or no opinion	12%	14%	12%	10%	25%	19%	33%	20%

Source: "Katko Maintains Double-Digit Lead Over Balter." Siena College Research Institute, October 28, 2018, https://scri.siena.edu/2018/10/28/katko-maintains-double-digit-lead-over-balter/

Table 3.35 Siena NY-24 poll: presidential approval rating

	Total	Democrats	Republicans	Ind./other
Approve	48%	18%	74%	48%
Disapprove	48%	79%	22%	47%
Don't know or no opinion	4%	3%	4%	5%

	Balter supporters	Katko supporters
Approve	3%	82%
Disapprove	96%	13%
Don't know or no opinion	1%	5%

Source: "Katko Maintains Double-Digit Lead Over Balter." Siena College Research Institute, October 28, 2018, https://scri.siena.edu/2018/10/28/katko-maintains-double-digit-lead-over-balter/

Table 3.36 Siena NY-24 poll: party control of house

	Total	Democrat	Republican	Ind./other
Democrat	44%	77%	15%	46%
Republican	49%	15%	78%	46%
Don't know or no opinion	7%	8%	7%	8%

	Balter supporters	Katko supporters
Democrat	93%	11%
Republican	1%	85%
Don't know or no opinion	6%	4%

Source: "Katko Maintains Double-Digit Lead Over Balter." Siena College Research Institute, October 28, 2018, https://scri.siena.edu/2018/10/28/katko-maintains-double-digit-lead-over-balter/

The Washington Post/Schar Survey conducted polling of 69 battleground House districts in October of 2018, including NY-19 and NY-22, enabling some comparison between these districts and battleground districts at large.[11] Sixty-three of these districts were controlled by Republicans and six by Democrats. President Trump won 48 of the districts in 2016. Hillary Clinton won 21. Trump's approval rating in battleground districts was 43 percent. This was lower than NY-19 (45 percent) and NY-22 (51 percent) at the same point in time.

Likely voters were split over supporting Democratic and Republican candidates, 48 percent supporting Democrats and 47 percent supporting Republicans. This was similarly reflected in extraordinarily close polling for candidates in NY-19 and NY-22. Women drove support for Democrats in battleground districts, preferring Democratic candidates 54 percent to 40 percent. This was reflected in NY-19, where Delgado had 52 percent support among women, and NY-22, where Brindisi had 51 percent.

Notes

1. "Faso leads Delgado by 5 points, 45–40," Siena College Research Institute, August 30, 2018, https://scri.siena.edu/2018/08/30/faso-leads-delgado-by-5-points-45-40-percent/
2. "New York: Voters Divided in CD19," Monmouth University Poll, September 12, 2018, https://www.monmouth.edu/polling-institute/documents/monmouthpoll_ny_091218.pdf/
3. "Separated By 1 Point: Faso 44%; Delgado 43%; Others 6%; Undecided 7%," Siena College Research Institute, October 22, 2018, https://scri.siena.edu/2018/10/22/new-york-19-oct-2018/
4. "Anthony Brindisi holds a double-digit lead over Claudia Tenney for the NY 22nd Congressional seat," Zogby Poll, May 2, 2018, https://zogby-analytics.com/news/844-the-zogby-poll-anthony-brindisi-holds-a-double-digit-lead-over-claudia-tenney-for-the-ny-22nd-congressional-seat-the-race-could-signal-dems-winning-back-the-house-of-representatives-millennials-women-and-independents-supporting-brindisi-over-tenney
5. "Incumbent Tenney and Challenger Brindisi Locked in Dead Heat," Siena College Research Institute, August 29, 2018, https://scri.siena.edu/2018/08/29/incumbent-tenney-challenger-brindisi-locked-in-a-near-dead-heat/
6. It is important to note this may be the result of differing polling techniques and is not necessarily attributable to shifts in public opinion.
7. Mark Weiner, "Is Donald Trump still the 'most popular person' ever in upstate New York?" *Syracuse.com*, August 12, 2018, https://www.syracuse.com/politics/index.ssf/2018/08/is_donald_trump_still_the_most_popular_person_ever_in_upstate_new_york.html
8. "New York 22: Brindisi 46%- Tenney 45%-Undecided 9%," *Siena Research Institute*, October 24, 2018, https://scri.siena.edu/2018/10/24/new-york-22-brindisi-46-tenney-45-undecided-9/
9. "Katko has 15 point Lead Over Balter, 54–39 percent," Siena College Research Institute, August 30, 2018, https://scri.siena.edu/2018/08/27/katko-has-15-point-lead-over-balter-54-39-percent/

10. "Katko Maintains Double-Digit Lead Over Balter." Siena College Research Institute, October 28, 2018, https://scri.siena.edu/2018/10/28/katko-maintains-double-digit-lead-over-balter/
11. Scott Clement and Dan Balz, "Survey of battleground House districts shows Democrats with narrow edge," *The Washington Post*, October 8, 2018, https://www.washingtonpost.com/politics/survey-of-battleground-house-districts-shows-democrats-with-narrow-edge/2018/10/07/f45e13f2-c812-11e8-b1ed-1d2d65b86d0c_story.html?utm_term=.430fd5fe7c4e

CHAPTER 4

Who Won and Why

Abstract This chapter examines who won the campaigns in NY-19, NY-22, and NY-24 and interprets the results.

Keyword Donald Trump • 2018 Midterm election • Party politics • Economy • Resistance • Grassroots organizing • John Katko • Anthony Brindisi • Antonio Delgado • Dana Balter • NY-19 • NY-22 • NY-24 • John Faso • Claudia Tenney

The midterm results in 2014 and 2018 reflect two very different presidencies and two very different outcomes. Turnout was 36 percent in 2014, the lowest in 70 years.[1] Vulnerable Democrats ran away from President Obama, who had an aggregate approval rating of 43 percent, and disapproval rating of 52 percent, and campaigned only sparingly.[2] Republicans took control of the U.S. Senate and expanded their majority in the House by 13 seats.[3]

Republicans did well in New York in the 2014 House elections. In Upstate New York, Republican challenger John Katko easily defeated Democratic incumbent Dan Maffei in NY-24. Elise Stefanik won an open seat election in NY-21, following the retirement of Democrat Bill Owens. Stefanik "campaigned as a cow milking local," while having worked in the

Bush administration and assisting Paul Ryan with his vice presidential campaign. Stefanik was the youngest woman ever elected to Congress at the age of 30, and was "considered a future star for the Republican Party."[4] Republican Lee Zeldin defeated Democratic incumbent Tim Bishop in NY-1, a rematch of the 2008 election. Republican incumbent Chris Gibson easily defeated Democratic challenger Sean Eldridge in NY-19.

In 2018, many Republicans embraced President Trump, who actively campaigned for House candidates, despite being identically unpopular as Obama in 2014, with a 42 percent job approval rating and 53 disapproval rating.[5] Democrats needed to gain 23 seats to take control of the House of Representatives and won 40. Turnout was 47 percent, a 50-year high for midterm elections.[6] Democrats did well in New York in the 2018 House elections. Three GOP House incumbents from New York were defeated "as part of a 'blue wave' that powered a Democratic takeover of the House."[7] Antonio Delgado defeated John Faso in NY-19. Anthony Brindisi defeated Claudia Tenney in NY-22. Max Rose defeated Dan Donovan in NY-11. Alexandria Ocasio-Cortez (NY-14) became the youngest woman ever elected to the House at the age of 29.

NY-11

Max Rose's upset victory NY-11, which includes Staten Island and a portion of Southern Brooklyn, unseated the only GOP House representative from New York City. Republican Dan Donovan was first elected in a 2015 special election following the resignation of Michael Grimm. Grimm was indicted on 20 counts related to the operation of his restaurant in Manhattan. Grimm pled guilty to one count of felony tax fraud and signed a "statement of facts" that acknowledged he committed perjury, hired illegal immigrants, and committed wire fraud.[8]

Grimm, who was reelected in 2014, while under indictment, initially declined to resign, though ultimately did so in January of 2015. Donovan, who was Staten Island District Attorney, easily won the subsequent special election in May of 2015, defeating Democrat Vincent Gentile, 60 percent to 39 percent. Donavan was the heavy favorite to retain the seat and "ran a cautious campaign, casting himself as a nonpartisan figure and adjusting his rhetoric according to circumstances."[9] Donovan was reelected in 2016, once again with over 60 percent of the vote, defeating Democratic challenger Richard Reichard.

Max Rose, a combat veteran in Afghanistan and former healthcare executive, distanced himself from some Democratic leaders, including Nancy Pelosi and New York City Mayor Bill de Blasio, while receiving endorsements from others, including Joe Biden, Governor Andrew Cuomo, and the Democratic Congressional Campaign Committee (DCCC), which included Rose in their Red-to-Blue program. Rose was aided by Grimm's challenge of Donavan in a bitterly contested Republican primary. Donavan, who prevailed with over 60 percent of the vote, ran as the preferred candidate of President Trump. After securing the Republican nomination, "Donavan's embrace of Mr. Trump was something less than full-throated." Donovan moved to the center in a district where Democrats outnumbered Republicans, though "skews heavily conservative."[10] Whether President Trump would hurt Donavan, more than help, was an issue "playing out across the country, but is particularly germane in New York City, where Mr. Trump was deeply unpopular."[11]

Richard Flanagan, Professor of Political Science at the College of Staten Island, described the general election campaign as a "scramble to the middle."[12] Republicans sought to portray Rose as a liberal progressive carpetbagger, while Donavan highlighted his public service roots in the district, from deputy borough president, to three-term District Attorney, to Congressman. Rose focused on local issues, including traffic congestion, poor subway service, and opioid addiction, seeking to appeal to Reagan Democrats, who "still exist on Staten Island," according to Flanagan.

Polling prior to the election was too close to call, though Donavan occasionally had a modest lead within the margin of error. Rose defeated Donovan 51 percent to 46 percent to become the first Democrat to represent the district in a decade.[13] Rose is among the youngest members of Congress at the age of 32.

NY-19

Antonio Delgado defeated John Faso by 7593 votes, 49 percent to 46 percent. Green Party Candidate Steve Greenfield won 4037 votes (1.51 percent) and Diane Neal won 2619 votes (just under 1 percent). Delgado did exceptionally well in Ulster County, the most populated county in the district, winning almost 60 percent of the vote for a nearly 16,000-vote advantage. This was a 5000 increase over Zephyr Teachout's performance in 2016. Delgado flipped Dutchess County, the second most populated county, and Columbia County, which Faso won in 2016, along with

Hillary Clinton. Turnout was high for a midterm election, exceeding 57 percent in every county, but Sullivan County.

Faso won the other eight counties in the district. Three of these counties (or partial counties) were sparsely populated comparatively speaking: Broome County, Otsego County, and Sullivan County. The five remaining counties netted over a 2000 vote advantage for Faso, but this was still well short of Delgado's advantage in Ulster County. Faso's margin of victory was down in every county he won, some considerably so. Faso fell over 2000 votes in six of the eight counties he won, including Delaware County, Green County, Otsego County, Rensselaer County, and Schoharie County (Tables 4.1, 4.2, 4.3, 4.4, and 4.5).

NY-22

Anthony Brindisi led Claudia Tenney by less than 1 percent on Election Night. Brindisi declared victory, as several prominent national news organizations called the election in his favor. Tenney spoke to supporters, but did not concede, though acknowledged trailing. Brindisi held a 1293 vote lead as absentee ballots were counted over the next several weeks. On November 20, Brindisi received a sufficient amount of absentee votes to win, which prompted Brindisi to declare victory, again.[14] Brindisi's campaign, which included Jordan Karp, a former election commissioner, left nothing

Table 4.1 NY-19 election night totals

Antonio Delgado	49.26% (132,001)
John Faso	46.42% (124,408)
Steve Greenfield	1.51% (4037)
Diane Neal	0.98% (2619)
Delgado's ballot lines	
Democratic Party	45.16%
Working Families Party	3.09%
Women's Equality Party	1.02%
Faso's ballot lines	
Republican Party	39.29%
Conservative Party	5.87%
Independence Party	1.04%
Reform Party	0.23%

Source: New York State Board of Elections, Unofficial Results, https://www.elections.ny.gov/2018ElectionResults.html

Table 4.2 NY-19 election day results by county

	Broome	Columbia	Delaware	Dutchess	Greene	Montgomery	Otsego
Antonio Delgado	36.76% 290	53.10% 13,897	40.54% 6408	49.49% 23,116	38.85% 7016	33.54% 1547	47.09% 9630
John Faso	58.81% 464	43.05% 11,268	55.12% 8713	46.37% 21,660	55.20% 9970	59.45% 2742	48.06% 9829

	Rensselaer	Schoharie	Sullivan	Ulster
Antonio Delgado	42.76% 12,018	36.12% 4189	46.97% 10,771	59.28% 43,119
John Faso	51.60% 14,502	58.79% 6819	49.10% 11,259	37.37% 27,182

Source: New York State Board of Elections, Unofficial Results, https://www.elections.ny.gov/2018ElectionResults.html

Table 4.3 NY-19 election day margin of victory by county

	Broome	Columbia	Delaware	Dutchess	Greene	Montgomery	Otsego
Antonio Delgado		+10.05% 2629		+3.12% 1456			
John Faso	+22.05% 174		+14.58% 2305		+16.35% 2954	+25.91% 1195	+0.97% 199

	Rensselaer	Schoharie	Sullivan	Ulster
Antonio Delgado				+21.91% 15,937
John Faso	+8.84% 2484	+22.67% 2630	+2.13% 488	

Source: New York State Board of Elections, Unofficial Results, https://www.elections.ny.gov/2018ElectionResults.html

to chance and targeted absentee voters as part of their efforts. Brindisi more than doubled his election night margin of victory to over 4000 votes after all additional ballots were counted,[15] and prevailed 50.4 percent to 49.6 percent.[16]

Turnout ranged by county from 50 percent in Cortland County to 60 percent in Madison County, with Oneida County and Broome County just under 60 percent. Brindisi's path to victory was built on flipping

Table 4.4 NY-19 election day voter turnout

	Total	Broome	Columbia	Delaware	Dutchess	Greene	Montgomery
Active registered voters	445,907	1363	44,186	26,801	76,014	29,737	7986
Number of voters	267,979	789	26,173	15,806	46,711	18,060	4612
Percent turnout	60%	57.8%	59.2%	58.9%	61.4%	60.7%	57.7%

	Otsego	Rensselaer	Schoharie	Sullivan	Ulster
Active registered voters	33,705	43,938	18,257	46,643	117,277
Number of voters	20,452	28,104	11,598	22,931	72,743
Percent turnout	60.6%	63.9%	63.5%	49.1%	62%

Source: New York State Board of Elections, Unofficial Results, https://www.elections.ny.gov/2018ElectionResults.html

Table 4.5 Comparing 2016 and 2018 NY-19 results

	2016 Presidential election	2016 House election	2018 House election
Broome	Trump +2%	Faso +396	Faso +174
Columbia	Clinton +5%	Faso +1437	Faso +2629
Delaware	Trump +26%	Faso +4914	Faso +2305
Dutchess	Clinton +less than 1%	Faso +2423	Delgado +1456
Greene	Trump +25%	Faso +6349	Faso +2954
Montgomery	Trump +24%	Faso +2072	Faso +1195
Otsego	Trump +11%	Faso +3047	Faso +199
Rensselaer	Trump +1%	Faso +7057	Faso +2484
Schoharie	Trump +33%	Faso +4011	Faso +2630
Sullivan	Trump +9%	Faso +1901	Faso +488
Ulster	Clinton +9%	Teachout +9545	Delgado +15,937

Source: Tables 1.7, 1.9, and 4.2

Oneida County. Tenney had a significant advantage there in 2016 facing Kim Myers, who is from Broome County. Brindisi did exceptionally well in Broome, the second most populated district, winning by 11 points. Myers was helpful in organizing on Brindisi's behalf during the campaign. Brindisi's large margin of victory in Broome, over 7000 votes, enabled him to withstand Tenney's victories in rural counties, such as Oswego County, Herkimer County, and Chenango County. Tenney won by double-digit margins in each, but the combined vote total was still shy of Brindisi's advantage in Broome County.

Tenney's margins of victory fell in every county she won. Diminished support was particularly noteworthy in Herkimer County and Madison County, where Tenney's advantage in each was cut by over half. This was not entirely unexpected in Madison County, where Trump's 2016 level of support was the lowest among counties Tenney won, though still a 14 point advantage. In contrast, Trump won Herkimer County by 33 points, his largest margin of victory in any NY-22 county (Tables 4.6, 4.7, 4.8, 4.9, and 4.10).

Table 4.6 NY-22 election night totals

Anthony Brindisi	49.51% (117,931)
Claudia Tenney	48.97% (116,638)
Brindisi's ballot lines	
Democratic Party	44.95%
Independence Party	2.22%
Working Families Party	1.82%
Women's Equality Party	0.52%
Tenney's ballot lines	
Republican Party	43.8%
Conservative Party	4.75%
Reform Party	0.42%

Source: New York State Board of Elections, Unofficial Results, https://www.elections.ny.gov/2018ElectionResults.html

Table 4.7 NY-22 election day results by county

	Broome	Chenango	Cortland	Herkimer	Madison	Oneida	Oswego
Anthony Brindisi	54.67%	42.69%	54.48%	43.86%	47.68%	50.13%	36.21%
	37,406	6803	8597	7792	11,745	38,263	5407
Claudia Tenney	43.47%	54.94%	44.17%	55.09%	50.97%	48.88%	60.96%
	29,742	8755	6970	9787	12,557	37,307	9103

	Tioga
Anthony Brindisi	43.56%
	1918
Claudia Tenney	54.89%
	2417

Source: New York State Board of Elections, Unofficial Results, https://www.elections.ny.gov/2018ElectionResults.html

Table 4.8 NY-22 election day margin of victory by county

	Broome	Chenango	Cortland	Herkimer	Madison	Oneida	Oswego
Anthony Brindisi	+11.20% 7664		+10.31% 1627			+1.25% 956	
Claudia Tenney		+12.25% 1952		+11.23% 1995	+3.29 812		+24.75% 3696

	Tioga
Anthony Brindisi	
Claudia Tenney	+11.33% 499

Source: New York State Board of Elections, Unofficial Results, https://www.elections.ny.gov/2018ElectionResults.html

NY-24

John Katko defeated Dana Balter by 15,174 votes, 52 percent to 46 percent. This was a much smaller margin than Katko's two previous victories and tighter than what polling indicated. Balter made significant inroads by flipping Onondaga County. Katko won the three other counties (Cayuga County, Oswego County, and Wayne County) with 59 percent vote share for over a 20-point advantage in each. Still, Katko's margins of victory were down compared to 2016. This was particularly pronounced in Wayne County, where Katko's advantage was cut by over half. Trump won Wayne County by 33 points in 2016, his largest margin of victory in any NY-24 county.

Fifty-seven percent of active voters turned out in NY-24. Turnout in Cayuga and Onondaga counties was a bit higher, while Wayne and Oswego counties were a bit lower. Each candidate received 43 percent of their vote total from their respective major party line. Katko had a clear advantage among the other ballot lines. The Conservative Party line and Independence Party line combined for 8 percent of his vote share. This nearly tripled Balter's vote share from the Working Families Party and Women's Equality Party line (Tables 4.11, 4.12, 4.13, 4.14, and 4.15).

Table 4.9 2018 NY-22 election day voter turnout

	Total	Broome	Chenango	Cortland	Herkimer	Madison	Oneida	Oswego
Active registered voters	405,396	114,074	27,939	28,242	31,529	41,018	128,377	27,107
Number of voters	238,195	68,416	15,936	15,779	17,764	24,634	76,330	14,933
Percent turnout	58.7%	59.9%	57%	50%	56.3%	60%	59.4%	55%

	Tioga
Active registered voters	7110
Number of voters	4403
Percent turnout	61.9%

Source: New York State Board of Elections, Unofficial Results, https://www.elections.ny.gov/2018ElectionResults.html

Table 4.10 Comparing 2016 and 2018 results in NY-22

	2016 Presidential election	2016 House election	2018 House election
Broome	Trump +2%	Myers +8794	Brindisi +7664
Chenango	Trump +25%	Tenney +3181	Tenney +1952
Cortland	Trump +6%	Myers +852	Brindisi +1627
Herkimer	Trump +33%	Tenney +4533	Tenney +1995
Madison	Trump +14%	Tenney +1806	Tenney +812
Oneida	Trump +20%	Tenney +3028	Brindisi +956
Oswego	Trump +22%	Tenney +4485	Tenney +3696
Tioga	Trump +26%	Tenney +791	Tenney +499

Source: Tables 1.10, 1.12, and 4.7

Table 4.11 2018 NY-24 election day results

John Katko	52.20% (129,276)
Dana Balter	46.08% (114,102)
Katko ballot lines	
Republican Party	43.31%
Conservative Party	6.45%
Independence Party	2.09%
Reform Party	0.36%
Balter ballot lines	
Democratic Party	43.35%
Working Families Party	1.8%
Women's Equality Party	0.93%

Source: New York State Board of Elections, Unofficial Results, https://www.elections.ny.gov/2018ElectionResults.html

Table 4.12 NY-24 election day results by county

	Cayuga	Onondaga	Oswego	Wayne
Dana Balter	38.32%	49.84%	37.99%	37.97%
	10,120	83,886	8556	11,540
John Katko	59.72%	48.73%	59.48%	59.55%
	15,771	82,007	13,396	18,102

Source: New York State Board of Elections, Unofficial Results, https://www.elections.ny.gov/2018ElectionResults.html

Table 4.13 2018 NY-24 election day margin of victory by county

	Cayuga	Onondaga	Oswego	Wayne
Dana Balter		+1.1% 1879		
John Katko	+21.40% 5651		+21.49% 4840	+21.58% 6562

Source: New York State Board of Elections, Unofficial Results, https://www.elections.ny.gov/2018ElectionResults.html

Table 4.14 Comparing 2016 and 2018 results in NY-24

	2016 Presidential election	2016 House election	2018 House election
Cayuga	Trump +11	Katko +10,799	Katko +5651
Onondaga	Clinton +14	Katko +30,112	Balter +1879
Oswego	Trump +22	Katko +8955	Katko +4840
Wayne	Trump +25	Katko 13,855	Katko +6562

Source: Tables 1.13, 1.15, and 4.12

Table 4.15 2018 NY-24 election day voter turnout

	Total	Cayuga	Onondaga	Oswego	Wayne
Active registered voters	429,161	45,408	287,261	41,803	54,689
Number of voters	247,632	26,410	168,305	22,521	30,396
Percent turnout	57.7%	58.1%	58.5%	53.8%	55.5%

Source: New York State Board of Elections, Unofficial Results, https://www.elections.ny.gov/2018ElectionResults.html

INTERPRETING THE RESULTS

Congressional election forecasters have long been divided by structuralists, who issue "forecasts from static, single equation explanatory models," and pollsters, who have increasingly relied on aggregate polling, the combination of several polls, to make electoral predictions about how House seats will change from one election to the next.[17] Synthesizers then merged structural models with aggregate polling, while a fourth dominant approach rejected standardization and relied on "whatever information they considered relevant," including qualitative and quantitative data.[18] This latter approach is most instructive in explaining the 2018 results in NY-19, NY-22, and NY-24.

In some ways, electoral outcomes fit with expectations. Two GOP inexperienced incumbents, John Faso and Claudia Tenney, lost in a difficult national political climate where they had problematically high unfavorable ratings, while the more popular two-term incumbent, John Katko, took a hit, but prevailed. On the other hand, if one focused on voter registration, Claudia Tenney would have been a presumed favorite, with a nearly 27,000 registered voter advantage of Republicans over Democrats, and John Katko, facing a 14,000 registered voter deficit of Democrats over Republicans, would have been picked off. This dichotomy helps to illustrate how the combination of candidate characteristics and external conditions combined to produce specific electoral outcomes.

Managing Trump

The president's party has lost an average of 25 House seats during midterm elections since 1946. Referendum theory posits that "presidents decline in popularity from their initial honeymoon period and the degree of popularity can matter at midterm."[19] The party of presidents polling under 50 percent loses 37 seats on average. The average loss falls to 14 seats when the president is above 50 percent.[20] Balance theory posits "the electorate boosts its support for the out party at midterm from a desire for balance in terms of ideology or policy."[21] Republicans took control of the House and state legislatures in 2010 and the Senate in 2014. Neither theory bode well for Republicans in 2018, who were predicted to lose the House.[22] President Trump was not popular compared to modern presidents heading into their first midterm. Trump had an aggregated approval rating of 41.8 percent on Election Day and 52.8 percent disapproval.[23] Republicans lost 40 seats in 2018, which is slightly above average for an unpopular president (Table 4.16).

Table 4.16 Presidential approval rating and midterm gains/losses

	Approval rating (prior to midterm)	*House seats lost/gained*
Barack Obama (2010)	45%	−63
George W. Bush (2002)	67%	+8
Bill Clinton (1994)	48%	−52
George H.W. Bush (1990)	57%	−8
Ronald Reagan (1982)	42%	−26
Jimmy Carter (1978)	45%	−15

Source: The American Presidency Project, http://www.presidency.ucsb.edu/data/mid-term_elections.php

Over the first two years of the Trump presidency some prominent Political Scientists concluded that Trump was a unique threat to U.S. democracy that should not be normalized.[24] This concern was even echoed by members of his administration. The *New York Times* published an anonymous editorial prior to the midterm by a "senior official" who claimed to be part of the resistance within the Trump administration. Dissension within a presidency is unremarkable and is often confined to isolated policy disagreements. Claiming to be part of a widespread opposition movement was unprecedented.[25]

Trump interjected himself into the 2018 midterm campaign like few other modern presidents have. This was harmful to House candidates in competitive districts, given Trump's unpopular and polarizing nature. The president held 20 campaign rallies during the summer and early fall of 2018 and made multiple campaign trips to various states.[26] Trump's total number of rallies exceeded 30, surpassing those by Presidents Obama and Bush, respectively.[27] In addition to public rallies, Trump also held dozens of private fundraisers for Congressional candidates across the country. This was more prudent and advantageous for Republican candidates.

Trump's rhetoric was deeply critical of Democrats, particularly toward the confirmation hearing of Brett Kavanaugh, and the prospect of being impeached, frequently including derogatory name-calling. Trump portrayed Republican candidates as dedicated to persevering law and order, securing the border, confirming conservative judges, and furthering the president's agenda. Trump explicitly asked voters to approach the election as if he were on the ballot, and sought to define the election as a choice between a strong economy, low unemployment, and low taxes, and his opponents, who want to "plunge our country into a nightmare of gridlock, poverty, chaos, and frankly, crime." "You don't hand matches to an arsonist," Trump explained at a rally in Iowa, "and you don't give power to an angry left-wing mob," which is "what the Democrats have become."[28]

The election unfolded in a moment of hyperpartisanship. Not surprisingly, partisan loyalty and dislike of the opposing parties and candidates were key factors in how people decided whom to vote for. Democratic voters were more motivated to vote against Republicans. Democrats were out of power following a presidential election where Donald Trump lost the popular vote, but the won the election, which was marked by a two year Justice Department investigation of collusion between his campaign and Russia. Nearly half of Republicans voters cast their vote in support of their party and candidates. Less than 30 percent did so in opposition to

Democrats. Democratic voters were evenly divided between supporting the party and opposing Republicans. President Trump galvanized Democratic opposition more than engendered Republican support. One in five Democratic voters cited opposition to President Trump as the main impetus for their vote. Just 1 in 10 Republican voters cited support for Trump as the main impetus of their vote.[29]

Given these dynamics, one of the most pivotal questions GOP incumbents faced in 2018 was how they would navigate the Trump presidency. Claudia Tenney unequivocally affixed her reelection path to the president's coattails. Trump outperformed Tenney in NY-22 by nine points, the second largest margin of victory the president had over any GOP House candidate in 2016. Tenney sought to expand her base, beyond the 46 percent she garnered in a three-way race, by running to the right, rather than the middle, or some combination of the two.

Tenney's embrace of the president took many forms. Tenney emulated Trump's deeply personal approach to politics, personally attacking anyone in or out of politics or her party she perceived to be a threat. Tenney hyperbolically lauded the administration. "Whether people like it or not," Tenney stated in May of 2018, "this is probably the most successful presidency in modern history as far what we've accomplished."[30] She arranged for Trump administration members to visit the district, including Ivanka Trump, advisor to the president, Linda McMahon, Administrator of the Small Business Administration, and Sonny Perdue, Secretary of Agriculture. Tenney believed these events were valuable opportunities for national officials to speak with constituent groups, like business owners and dairy farmers. During the campaign, Donald Trump came to Utica to campaign and fundraise for Tenney, as did Eric Trump, Donald Trump Jr., and Sarah Huckabee Sanders.

At the same time, like Trump, Tenney frequently struggled to stay on message during the campaign. A prominent example was her official reelection launch. She grew frustrated with a reporter who asked about her mass murder comment and the Russia investigation. She leaned into the small press pool and screamed: "It's fake news! I answered your question every which way. It's fake news." Tenney then abruptly walked off and refused to talk more with the media.[31]

Tenney also promoted conspiracy theories embraced by the president. For instance, she stated in March of 2015 that voter fraud is "a very real issue" that needed to be addressed, claiming turnout in U.S. elections exceeded 100 percent in various places around the country. This was propagated online following the 2012 presidential election, typically in support of Voter ID laws. *Politifact* debunked the assertion in Florida,[32] Pennsylvania,[33] and Ohio,[34] and related claims.[35] Similar sentiments were expressed by Donald Trump, who claimed the electoral system was "rigged" prior to the 2016 election, which were also debunked,[36] as were his assertions that five millions noncitizens voted in 2016.[37]

Tenney also perpetuated the conception of the "deep state," lifetime government employees devoted to working against President Trump. In March of 2018, she defended Ben Carson, Secretary of Housing and Urban Development, as he faced scrutiny for using $31,000 of public funds on an office dining set for private lunches. Tenney claimed that "somebody in the deep state" ordered the furniture, not one of Carson's staff.[38]

Tenney defended the president and his campaign staff as they were indicted and pled guilty to federal crimes, at times in ways that were inaccurate and/or untruthful. "A lot of people aren't happy with the fact we're convicting one person after another," Tenney said in August of 2018 after Paul Manafort, Trump's former campaign advisor, pled guilty to eight counts of fraud, "and we've yet to discover any kind of so-called collusion, which isn't a crime anyway." *Politifact* found this assertion, one commonly made by Trump and his legal team, to be "mostly false."[39] Tenney also claimed that what Michel Cohen "pled guilty to didn't have anything to do with the president." Cohen committed two counts of campaign finance law violations related to his work for Trump as well as six counts of tax and bank fraud.[40]

In April of 2018, Tenney was among 11 House Republicans who requested federal investigations of James Comey, Hillary Clinton, Loretta Lynch, Andrew McCabe, Peter Strzok, and Lisa Page. This came after Comey, a former FBI director who Trump fired, provided Congressional testimony widely considered damaging to the president. A joint letter was sent to Attorney General Jeff Sessions, FBI Director Christopher Wray, and U.S. Attorney John Huber, requesting they investigate "potential violation(s) of federal statutes" and identifying specific behaviors of each individual in relation to perceived violations of federal law. The signatories, including Tenney, wanted Comey investigated for perjury and falsehoods.[41] The Justice Department did not act on the request.

Tenney and Trump were tightly aligned all the way to Election Day. Trump tweeted one a last appeal for support the night before: "I need @claudiatenney of #NY22 to be re-elected in order to get our big plans moving. Her opponent would be a disaster. Nobody works harder than Claudia, and she is a producer. I look forward to working together with her—she has my Strongest Endorsement! Vote Claudia!"[42] Tenney's overwhelming alignment with Trump proved to be a fundamental miscalculation that doomed her reelection prospects. If she brought Republican moderates back into the fold, she would have won.

John Katko took the opposite approach of Tenney, reflecting different strategic and personal considerations. NY-24 was a much more Democratic district, where Hillary Clinton won by three points. Katko did not depend on Trump to become a Congressman and offered no political loyalty to him. Katko did not vote for him in 2016 and was disinterested in Trump's endorsement in 2018. Katko stated in August of 2018, "I am an independent person, I am a bipartisan person and I want to do what's right for my constituents. I don't think endorsements matter all that much."[43] He went on to make clear that he was "not seeking anyone's endorsement at that level" and really didn't care if Trump endorsed him or not.

The two were clearly at odds professionally. Katko regularly referenced his background as a former federal prosecutor in supporting rule of law and the U.S. Justice Department. Unlike Tenney, Katko consistently defended the Mueller investigation and rejected the notion it was "a witch hunt." "When people around you are starting to get themselves convicted," Katko explained, "that's obviously a point of concern" and "why the Mueller investigation must continue."[44] He called for the Mueller investigation to be completed unimpeded by political pressure from elected officials, including the White House, who is "not above the law." Katko did not think legislation to protect the investigation was necessary, but was open to this if the president sought to stop the investigation.

Katko was widely supportive of more traditional Republican principles, supporting tax cuts and prioritizing national security. Per *Five Thirty Eight,* Katko voted in line with President Trump 90 percent of the time, similar to John Faso (89 percent), and lower than Claudia Tenney (97 percent), yet 30 points higher than expected given the nature of district.[45] In doing so, Katko supported several aspects of the president's agenda, most notably the tax cut, as previously discussed, and deregulation. He supported the Financial Choice Act, which rolled back portions of Dodd-Frank Act adopted in response to the Great Recession, and legislation that revoked internet privacy rules established by the Federal Communications Commission.[46] Katko also backed some of Trump's environmental deregulation efforts, including repealing the Stream Protection Rule that sought to protect waterways from mountaintop removal mining the president claimed was part of the "war on coal." At the same time, he at times bucked the president in regards to the environment, joining ten other

House Republicans who opposed the party's successful efforts to repeal regulations that reduced methane emissions from oil and gas drilling on public lands.

Katko sought to manage his policy support of the president's agenda by highlighting areas of disagreement. As previously discussed, healthcare was a prominent example. He was also critical of the president regarding immigration, for his lack of leadership and good faith negotiation surrounding Katko's efforts to pass the Border Security and Immigration Act. Katko believed "if the president had said from the beginning, 'This is a great bill, you guys all need to get behind it,' it would have passed the House. But he equivocated because he listened to those guys chirping at him. And I think that was a huge mistake."[47]

When asked in September of 2018 if he had any concerns about the fitness or ability of President Trump to fulfill his responsibilities," Katko replied, "No, I fully believe in checks and balances." Katko supported and criticized presidents based on the merits and has "no blanket hate or dislike of anyone" of them.[48] This aptly sums up his arm's-length approach to President Trump. Katko was able to successfully retain the backing of Trump supporters, while sufficiently convincing moderate Republicans and independents he was bipartisan and not overly tied to any person or party.

John Faso was less supportive of President Trump than Tenney, but less critical of him than Katko. This middle-ground approach ultimately fell short in a swing district that moved leftward following 2016 when Faso was elected. As previously discussed, Faso voted in favor of the American Health Care Act, but against the tax cut because of the State and Local Tax Deduction cap. Russia was a main source of Faso's criticism of Donald Trump. In March of 2018, Faso expressed disappointment about the Trump administration's handling of Russia. Faso thought "we need to be much more forthright about the fact that the Russians have malign intentions toward the United States."[49] In July of 2018, Faso criticized the president for a press conference with Vladimir Putin in which Trump stated that he did not think Russia meddled in the 2016 election. Faso released the following statement in response:

> I do not agree with the approach taken by President Trump at today's press conference with Russian President Vladimir Putin. Putin is no friend to the United States. There is no credibility to Putin's denials especially in light of the public evidence and our own U.S. intelligence reports. We know the Russians meddled in our elections and we must continue our sanctions and diplomatic pressure against Putin's actions.[50]

President Trump did not come to NY-19 to campaign or fundraise for Faso, but did endorse him in October of 2018. Trump tweeted on Election Day: "Strong on Crime, Borders and our 2nd Amendment, John is respected by all. Vote for John. He has my complete and total Endorsement!"[51]

The next day President Trump declared "very close to complete victory" in the midterm election, even though Republicans lost the House, and selectively lambasted unsuccessful GOP incumbents for not sufficiently embracing his presidency and/or seeking his assistance on the campaign trail.[52] Trump singled out individuals by name, including Faso, who described the president's remarks as "unfortunate." Faso did not think embracing Trump more would have helped him win. NY-19 was "very divided" and the Democratic base was "energized."[53] Faso said that there was "no doubt the president has strong support within the Republican Party," but the party has to "recognize the tone sometimes is going to turn off some voters."[54]

Faso felt like he "was going to win right up until 10 p.m. on election night." "I had told my wife earlier in the summer that if we lost 20 seats in the house," Faso explained, "we would most likely win," but "if we lost 40 seats in the House, we would lose."[55] He believed that nationwide opposition to Trump was an unhelpful factor beyond his control. Faso viewed this as "a real warning and a wake-up call to the president and administration and Republicans generally." "The party is in trouble," he explained, "and it is something that has been coming for a long time. If you look at demographics and enrollment patterns across the state. ... We really have to do self-analysis on this question." Faso praised Trump's judicial nominations and economic deregulation efforts, but criticized the president's approach. Faso said many Republicans are concerned "by the daily chaos and the personality issues that surrounded the president and the White House," and wished Trump "wouldn't say a lot of what he says."[56] Faso concluded that Trump "was a decidedly negative factor in my race and races across the country where we lost the House" and that "it's fair to say his prospects in 2020 are very uncertain."[57]

The Economy

The positive state of the economy was one remarkable element of Republican's losing the House. Conventional thinking is that elected officeholders tend to be rewarded in good economic times. This was certainly not the case in 2018. Political Scientists are divided over the extent to which the state of the economy influences midterm electoral outcomes for the House. This appears to be more of the case during the nineteenth and twentieth centuries than today, because of factors such as diminished Congressional power in economic policymaking and the dominance of local issues on House campaigns.[58] Still, the state of the economy is a predominant focus of structural election models, and was a significant consideration during the Great Recession, though scholars differ on how best to measure this variable as it relates to voter decision-making.[59]

By all accounts, the economy was doing well during the 2018 campaign cycle. Economic growth was 4.2 percent in the second quarter of 2018, from July to September, and 3.5 percent in the third quarter, ending in late November.[60] Unemployment was at 3.7 percent, the lowest rate since 1969.[61] The economy was identified as the country's most important problem by just 13 percent of likely voters, a historically low amount. During the Great Recession (2007–2009), 86 percent identified the economy as the top problem, and even five years later, during the last midterm in 2014, 53 percent of likely voters held this view (Fig. 4.1).

In 2018 the economy ranked fourth in terms of important issues, behind healthcare, immigration, and taxes, but ahead of 14 other issues, including some that were prominent during the campaign, such as gun policy and opioid addiction. Seventy-four percent of voters said the issue was "very important" to their votes. This sentiment was more pronounced among Democrats (85 percent) than Republicans (66 percent).[62] Jobs were not as paramount a concern as other issues. Trade policy, immigration policy, and taxes were more prevalent.[63]

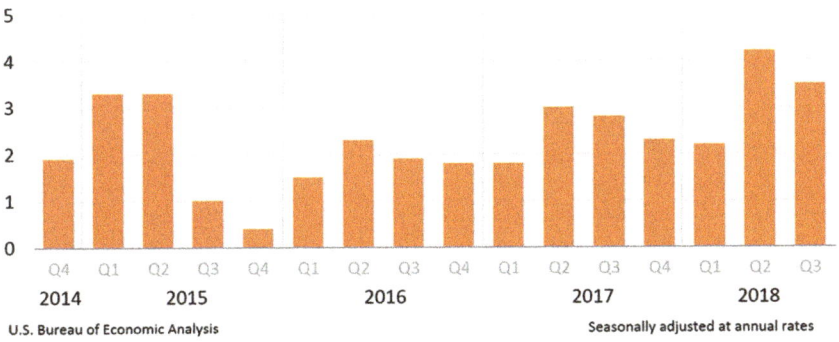

Fig. 4.1 Real GDP: percent change from preceding quarter

The question of who was benefiting from a robust economy became a related theme, particularly among Democrats. Wages have not kept pace with inflation, while American-spending patterns illustrated how the bottom 60 percent of income earners were "essentially drawing on their savings just to maintain their lifestyles" because "their incomes weren't enough to cover expenses."[64] A range of Americans still felt "far from financially secure even nine years into an economic expansion," facing challenges such as a lack of affordable housing, childcare costs, and high gas prices.[65]

Still, Americans consistently approved of President Trump's handling of the economy.[66] Trump frequently spoke about the economy at campaign rallies, and tweeted about it, in a credit-claiming manner. Why weren't Republicans able to capitalize on a robust economy? President Trump's unorthodox messaging created unique challenges for Republican candidates. Trump needlessly overstated the positive state of the economy, prompting fact-checking and ridicule.[67]

"Theoretically, the economy should take some of the edge off Democratic gains," observed David Wasserman from the Cook Political Report, but "the problem for Republicans is President Trump, who frequently dominates the headlines with non-economic news."[68] While Trump frequently spoke about the economy, he spoke nearly as frequently about immigration in the closing weeks, a more polarizing issue that played to his base better than the rest of the political spectrum.[69]

CANDIDATE QUALITY

The 2018 House elections in Central New York illustrated how candidates matter. John Katko entered the 2018 campaign as the most experienced of the three GOP incumbents examined here, both in terms of serving in Congress and competing in Congressional campaigns. Katko built a larger political base, winning twice with 60 percent of the vote. Claudia Tenney and John Faso were elected just once with 46 percent and 54 percent of the vote, respectively. Generating Democratic support has long been one important component of Katko's electoral success. While Katko received less Democrat votes in 2018 than in the past, "it's clear he received some support from the other side," including in Democratic strongholds of the district, such as Auburn, which has an all-Democratic council and Democratic mayor.[70] This was particularly important as Democratic turnout around the country was higher this midterm than the last. This also illustrates the existence of moderate Democrats, who, faced with a choice between Katko or a more progressive Democrat, chose the former.

A second component to Katko's success was the strength of his messaging and voter mobilization efforts. Katko's ground game is "a big reason why he wins elections," though one easily overlooked in previous landslide victories, "and it helped him win again this year."[71] Katko relied on strong relationships with local GOP officials to galvanize rural and suburban turnout in his favor. This was pivotal in the face of enthusiastic grassroots support for Balter, who wisely campaigned throughout the district, evening where she would lose, avoiding the pitfalls of a too Syracuse-centric approach.

Balter was hampered by the DCCC's decision to put Juanita Perez Williams in their Red-to-Blue Program, ahead of the primary. In NY-19, the DCCC included Delgado in the program after he became the nominee. Balter was a first time candidate, with little name recognition, who initially struggled to raise money. Perez Williams was a 2017 mayoral candidate in Syracuse and furthered national party efforts to embody diversity, as the granddaughter of Mexican immigrants. The problem was that all four Democratic county committees already endorsed Balter when the DCCC supported Perez Williams. The committees issued a joint statement that accused the DCCC of not taking "into account the work happening at the grass roots this year," reiterated their support for Balter and criticized DCCC "meddling that has hampered far too many races thus far."[72] This was clearly not helpful for Balter, who had a very narrow path to victory to begin with.

John Katko enjoyed a significant fundraising advantage initially. Balter's campaign was outraised by Katko $1.4 million to $193,000 by the end of May in 2018.[73] This was in part due to primary uncertainties. Democratic donors were reluctant to give money until they knew who the nominee was. Moreover, Balter had to spend most of what she raised to help secure the nomination. To her credit, Balter was well organized from the outset and easily won the primary, even though polls showed her trailing.[74] Afterward, Balter shattered the NY-24 record for fundraising in a quarter—over $1.5 million between July 1 and September 30. Katko's best quarter was $525,105. Democratic candidate Dan Maffei previously held the highest quarter mark at $592,663 in 2008. Balter finished with fundraising totals that exceeded Maffei and Katko when they were challengers in 2006 ($958,298) and 2014 ($1,029,766), respectively. Balter's campaign also exceeded the best NY-24 fundraising cycle of Jim Walsh, who raised $1,396,424 in 2006 as an incumbent. Her prodigious fundraising erased Katko's monetary advantage. By late October of 2018, Balter's campaign had more cash-on-hand than Katko for the first time, $621,383 to $529,874.[75]

Though Balter lost, she emerged from the campaign a significantly stronger candidate than when she first declared in September of 2017. Name recognition, campaign experience, and fundraising abilities were transformed from liabilities into assets. Balter also proved to be an exceptional debater with solid command of the issues, poise, and excellent verbal communication skills. Increased turnout, winning Onondaga County, and narrowing Katko's margin of victory to within striking distance are building blocks for another campaign in 2020. Balter was not ready to declare following the 2018 election, but hinted that may happen, as she pledged to stay active in local politics. "Obviously that's something that's incredibly important to me," she explained. "I think we've built a really powerful movement and I have no intention of walking away from that."[76]

Anthony Brindisi was clearly the most talented and formidable candidate Democrats could run in NY-22. Brindisi had established roots in Oneida County and electoral experience at the state and local level. Local party leaders, who served for decades, spoke highly of his extraordinary, natural abilities to connect with people. Political operatives cited Brindisi's student-like approach to learning policy particulars and credited him as the source of innovative campaign maneuvers, such as turning Spectrum Cable into a campaign issue. His campaign consistently focused on local issues and purposefully hired staff from within the district.

Brindisi declared his candidacy just months into Tenney's first term, mostly to raise money. Conventional wisdom suggested Tenney's seat on the House Financial Services Committee was a boon for campaign fundraising, though Brindisi proved himself to be the superior fundraiser. Tenney was 1 of 16 GOP incumbents in 62 competitive races outraised by challengers in 2017.[77]

Brindisi's campaign outraised Tenney's campaign each quarter of 2018 as well. Donald Trump's fundraiser in Utica raised about $150,000 for Tenney, but Brindisi still outraised her that quarter, well exceeding $1 million, the first time either candidate had done so. Tenney received much more PAC money and money from outside of the state and district than Brindisi. Seventy-five percent of Tenney's donations exceeded $1000 compared to 45 percent for Brindisi. Three-quarters of Brindisi's donations came from within New York State compared to 41 percent for Tenney. Thirty percent of Brindisi's donations came from NY-22, more than double that of Tenney, 13 percent.[78]

Tenney did not have a strong campaign or local network to rely on. Tenney was outspoken about bucking the Republican establishment and first sought the NY-22 seat as an unsuccessful Tea Party challenger to incumbent Richard Hanna, a bitter race Hanna won. Hanna retired in 2016, in part because the Republican Party had moved right, and it was unclear if he would survive another primary challenge. This provided an opening for Tenney, though she was not the top choice of the National Republican Congressional Committee (NRCC) or the clear frontrunner. Tenney won a three-way primary in 2016 with 41 percent of Republican support, but her margin of victory was only 1564 votes, as most Republicans voted for Steve Wells (34 percent) or George Phillips (25 percent).

Tenney never fully consolidated Republican support and publicly touted she was elected without the endorsement of county GOP committees. This was not helpful to her reelection prospects, particularly in a two-way race against a formidable Democratic challenger. Tenney's campaign also mismanaged opportunities to build internal support. She successfully brought a sitting U.S. president to Utica, no small accomplishment, but did so in manner that generated local tension, publicly and privately. Tenney denied a request by the Mayor of Utica, Robert Palmieri (D), to greet the president, claiming it was a fundraising trip, not an official visit. Tenney's campaign then refused to pay for the police and other services required for the president's visit and personally criticized the mayor.[79] Behind the scenes, local Republican leaders were not well informed of about Trump's fundraiser. The timing and location were kept secret until purchasing a ticket. Tenney's campaign initially sent out an e-mail to supporters explaining there would be no comps, which left local Republican activists wondering what their $1000–15,000 ticket would get them. Making matters worse, Tenney's campaign offered select individuals half-price tickets days before the event, but did not include all local party leaders. As a whole, this was a missed opportunity to engender support from party volunteers and activists whose enthusiasm and mobilization would be necessary for Tenney to prevail.

Lack of information and lack of access was also an ongoing challenge for some party leaders during Tenney's tenure, even ones who were generally inclined to help her. Tenney's inability to stay on message was a paramount concern for these Republicans, who encouraged Tenney to focus on her record. Tenney made many controversial statements while in office, which generated unfavorable attention locally and nationally. Most notably, in February of 2018, Tenney claimed without evidence that "it's interesting that so many of these people that commit the mass murders end up being Democrats. But the media doesn't talk about that."[80] The comment prompted Larry Sabato, prominent Political Scientist and election forecaster, to ask: "[I]s this not one of the dumbest, most inappropriate comments ever?"[81] To make matters worse, Tenney continued to defend the comment publicly, while privately admonishing local Republicans for not supporting her, because in her view, she was helping them.

Tim Byrnes, Professor of Political Science at Colgate University, was "taken aback by the brazen, and apparently purposeful, nature of Tenney's attacks on civility, truth telling and professional behavior," even by the standards of being a fairly jaded observer of politicians and their self-dealing. "Whether it was Tenney's intemperate approach to civic conflict (calling Oneida Indian Ray Halbritter 'Spray Tan Ray'), her bizarre misrepresentation of the budgetary effects of tax cuts (economic growth means the tax cuts have already paid for themselves), or her mean spirited attempts to exploit murderous tragedies for partisan advantage (serial killers tend to be Democrats)," Byrnes said. "Tenney has led the Congressional way in the spread of Trumpian misinformation and debased discourse."[82] Tenney was a polarizing political figure not only within the district, but within the Republican Party as well.

Nowhere in New York were "Democratic prospects for victory greater than in the 19th district."[83] The first challenge for Antonio Delgado was to overcome a contested seven-way primary in which six candidates won double-digit support. Delgado won by 1635 votes or 4 percent, defeating Pat Ryan, an Iraq War Veteran and small business owner, and Gareth Rhodes, a former staffer for Governor Cuomo, 22 percent to 18 percent, respectively. Intraparty divisions, which were tense down the stretch, healed quickly as factions put aside their differences to support the successful nominee. In some ways, the excitement and early start on the campaign was beneficial for Democrats, who were better prepared to advocate and mobilize.

Delgado became a formidable challenger in the general election "with his charismatic oratory style, grassroots appeal, and fundraising prowess."[84] Faso struggled to disqualify Delgado as a carpetbagger, who defined his life story through his family and middle-class upbringing in the district. Faso's emphasis on his three decades of work and service to the region helped fuel a perception "of Faso as something a white, suburban, 'country club' figure."[85]

This was not helpful with Donald Trump in the White House, a leftward shifting district, and an opponent who resembled Barack Obama more than Trump or Hillary Clinton.

Delgado outraised his competitors during the primary and general election.[86] Between January of 2017 through October of 2018, Delgado raised $6,589,846 to Faso's $3,334,925, for a nearly two-to-one advantage.[87] One-third of total fundraising from both candidates came from outside New York. Three-quarters came from outside of the district. A much larger portion of Faso's contributions came from PACs, 35 percent, compared to 7 percent for Delgado. The vast majority of Faso's PAC money came from corporate PACs, while most of his donations overall came from the financial sector. Delgado, Brindisi, and Balter all pledged to not accept corporate PAC money. Many of Delgado's large donations, those over $1000, came from employees at his former law firm, Akin Gump, who was "by far his single biggest source of fundraising."[88]

Unlike Katko, Faso was unable to effectively maintain a coalition of Republicans, independents, and moderate Democrats within an increasingly Democratic district. Unlike Tenney, Faso blamed Donald Trump for the Democratic victory in the House that swept him out of office. Unlike both of his GOP colleagues, Faso was outspoken that the election should be very concerning for Republicans and President Trump looking ahead to Republican prospects in 2020.

GRASSROOTS ORGANIZING

President Trump engendered a unique opposition movement purposely self-titled "the resistance" that bolstered Democratic candidates around the country and in Central New York. The intensification and mobilization of liberal grassroots organizations began immediately after Trump's inauguration with the historic Women's March, "the largest single-day demonstration recorded in U.S. history."[89] The ranks of existing liberal organizations grew, while new organizations emerged.

Indivisible arguably had the biggest electoral impact in 2018. The organization centered itself around a "practical guide to resist the Trump agenda" in leading "a movement of thousands of group leaders and more than a million members taking regular, iterative, and increasingly complex actions to resist the GOP's agenda, elect local champions, and fight for progressive policies."[90] Indivisible viewed the Trump presidency as an existential threat to democracy, which they sought to save. Their focus was civic education and campaigning. The latter included "empowering Indivisible groups to achieve legislative and electoral victories through legislative advocacy and political campaign expertise, strategic and coordinated calls to action, and a targeted electoral program" while "providing Indivisible groups access to voter contact software, along with a suite of canvassing, phonebanking, and texting tools in support of progressive candidates."[91] The *Indivisible Guide* was read by many founders of local grassroots resistance groups, such as *Sister District, Run for Something, Action Together, Swing Left*, and *Women's March*, who have hired staff and sought to cultivate and coordinate more local activism.[92] These national organizations provided the spark for thousands of "pop-up" organizations with "inchoate volunteer armies" who provided "reliable support for campaign practicalities like door-knocking and phone-banking, tasks that lacked the glamour and solidarity of marches and protests."[93]

Special Congressional elections in 2017 provided the first electoral test for organizers. Several of these elections were held to fill seats vacated by members of Congress joining the Trump administration. Openings typically emerged in consistently conservative parts of the country. Scandal was a key variable that helped some races become competitive. In Montana's at large House district, for instance, Republican-favorite Greg Gianforte was charged with assaulting a reporter. "The Republican National Committee took no chances and deployed Mike Pence with pre-recorded phone call to mobilize supporters," even though Gianforte was polling with a double-digit lead heading into the election.[94] Gianforte won by six points.

Republicans were less successful in Alabama's special election to fill the U.S. Senate Seat vacated by Jeff Sessions. Doug Jones became the first Democratic Alabama Senator since 1996 after defeating Roy Moore in a remarkable upset. Moore was a three-point favorite in the polls before Election Day, though he faced allegations of sexual assault of girls, which became a national story in the last month of the campaign. Jones, who won by one point, was propelled to victory "a massive coordinated mobilization apparatus deployed on the ground," which included "a compilation of national grass-roots organizations that partnered with local chapter groups like the NAACP."[95] African-American turnout was 29 percent, higher than normal, as "black voters came to the polls with unexpected and unheralded zeal."[96] How Democrats did this "offered a roadmap for 2018," given "the inertia of voter suppression and Republican domination in a racially polarized state."[97]

Groups, such as a *Woke Vote*, gathered students, churchgoing activists, and election organizers, and differed from traditional Democratic mobilization efforts by operating independently from parties and candidates.[98] *Woke Vote* illustrated how grassroots liberal organizations supplemented existing party and candidate campaign structures. Doug Jones did not actively court black voters, fearing that racial appeals would alienate white rural voters. These organizations focused on centers of black political power, such as historically black churches and colleges and universities. Organizers sought to turn potential new voters into force-multipliers by encouraging them to become organizers as well. This was done by having people not only pledge to vote, but bring others with them. Other groups, such as *BlackPAC*, provided practical guidance for how to navigate Alabama election law and deployed lawyers to the polls on Election Day to address irregularities. Canvassing efforts were more involved than distributing literature and included, for instance, how to get necessary identification to vote, if they needed it. *BlackPAC* found it particularly helpful to hire organizers, rather than solely relying on volunteers. This "tactic helped offset the strain and demands of canvassing rural and hard-to-reach communities in the state."[99] The end result was an expanded electorate in a state with some of the most demanding voter laws in the country.

Some scholars, such as Theda Skocpol, have compared the Tea Party movement to liberal grassroots organizing after the 2016 election. The Tea Party bolstered GOP electoral prospects from 2009 to 2011 by "pulling the Republican Party toward an uncompromising position" and providing a "basis at the grassroots level for Trump to emerge."[100] The movement was inherently undisciplined and constituted "a convergence of top-down and bottom-up forces." Nine-hundred local Tea Party organizations were formed at the grassroots level, which impacted local GOP party committees, by pressuring candidates and officeholders, and galvanized conservatives to vote in Republican primaries. The Tea Party did not employ big regional marches like post-Trump grassroots organizing. People got involved through a mix of personal interaction (e.g. meeting at a demonstration), media (e.g. reading a letter-to-the-editor), and digital connection (e.g. Meetup was used to connect people). These techniques were similar to what Indivisible advised people to do. Another parallel was that both conservative and liberal grassroots efforts were heavily contingent on volunteers, most of whom were people who had some flexibility in their schedules, such as stay-at-home-Moms or small business owners.[101]

Women were central to anti-Trump grassroots organizing, tens of thousands of whom, "mostly mothers and grandmothers ranging in age from their 30s to 70s, were fueling an American political transformation that most media outlets are systematically missing, or at least misreading."[102] While much attention was granted to the Women's Marches and a high number of female Democratic challengers in 2018, there was "a deeper and broader shift powering these indicators, and those who see only nationally visible events may miss it entirely. Far from the bluest strongholds, a huge demographic swathe of forgotten Americans was remaking politics." Half of Americans live in suburbs, double those who live in fully urban or rural communities. "Americans are also women—and of those, half are in their thirties to sixties. It is in this Middle America, and among these Middle Americans, that political developments since the November 2016 election have moved fastest and farthest."[103]

Ideologically, these predominately college-educated, suburban white women were "not a leftist Tea Party." They represented a range of viewpoints from the center to left of the political spectrum. The dynamic was different from the 2016 Democratic primary pitting Hillary Clinton against Bernie Sanders and Occupy Wall Street. Organizers moved on to confront the political realities of the Trump presidency and believe in good governance and strengthening Democratic norms. The dynamic was also different from the 1960s as many older Americans led the way in 2018, while "there are lots of helpful teenagers in the background saying, 'Mom, it's fine: go to your meeting; I'll get dinner myself.'"[104]

There were two general theories among Democrats about how to win the House in 2018: turnout the liberal base or appeal to moderates. Democrats did both and won the overall popular vote in House election by seven points. Democrats did well in districts that voted for Hillary Clinton in 2016, but also had a GOP House incumbent. This underscores the challenge faced and overcome by John Katko.

Conversely, progressive Democratic candidates, "who attempted to win districts by appealing to the left's base and running on issues like Medicare-for-all didn't fare as well" as their moderate Democratic counterparts.[105] This played out in Central New York as Dana Balter was more progressive than Antonio Delgado, whose district was more Democratic, and Anthony Brindisi, whose district was much more Republican. Other examples of progressive House candidates who lost were Scott Wallace (PA-1), Leslie Cockburn (VA-5), and Kara Eastman

(NE-2). At the same time, the Congressional Progressive Caucus gained several "high-profile new members," most notably Alexandria Ocasio-Cortez (NY-14), as well as Ayanna Pressley (MA-7), Deb Haaland (NM-1), Rashida Tlaib (MI-13), and Ilhan Omar (MN-5).[106]

Progressive candidates ran and won more primaries than ever before, but progressives remained one faction of the party. The party's base was "fired up about left-wing policies," while "many of its candidates were busy trying to reach across the aisle."[107] Democrats traded "ideological purity for electoral viability in many campaigns, much more so than the Republican Party, which moved farther to the right as a plurality of Republican voters now consider themselves "very conservative.'"[108] This was on display in NY-22, where Brindisi seemed "an imperfect choice" for Democrats "given the leftward tilt of progressive groups that have sprung up across Central New York in the wake of the Trump presidency."[109] As previously discussed, Brindisi long had an "A" rating from the National Rifle Association, pledged not to support Nancy Pelosi as Speaker, and "devoted more airtime to burnishing his bipartisan credentials than he does to criticizing President Trump."[110] Yet Democrats quickly unified behind a centrist Democrat who was the strongest challenger to Claudia Tenney. "Our hashtag is #OneTermTenney," explained Sarah Reeske, co-leader of Indivisible Mohawk Valley, citing the motto of Knit the District, a coalition of grassroots organizations formed in April of 2017. Reeske believed that Brindisi was "not 'Republican Lite' by any means," but truly independent.[111]

Knit the District was formed to foster relationships and collaboration among liberal organizers, support progressive candidates, defeat Claudia Tenney, help educate each other and share best practices. The coalition included Indivisible Mohawk Valley, Madison/Chenango Call to Action, Indivisible Madison County NY-22, Cazenovia Call to Action, Indivisible Cortland County, Indivisible Binghamton, and Chenango Change. Members from these organizations were a substantial portion of Brindisi's volunteers, a significant factor in a district where Republicans significantly outnumber Democrats, and maximizing turnout is essential. In addition to volume, timing and duration were also important considerations. Organizers became active shortly after Tenney's first term began. They participated in Indivisible trainings, fleshed out organizational structures that fit their goals, developed a close relationship with Brindisi, and consulted with local Democratic Party committees.

The Democratic Party assigned a staff member to work closely with grassroots volunteers. This person, Jon Lipe, who later joined Brindisi's campaign, was instrumental in developing relationships with resistance groups, helping them define success, and preparing members to become campaign volunteers. This began by earning their trust and then teaching vital campaign skills, including how to phone bank, canvass, and use VAN, a voter data base and web-hosting service provider used by the Democratic Party. Many activists ran for local office in 2017, often unsuccessfully, or helped with related campaigns. This was a practice run for 2018 and illustrated the work and difficulty involved with electing a Democratic Congressional candidate in a Republican district.

Throughout election year, grassroots organizers engaged in extensive canvassing efforts, heavily engaged various forms of media, and organized protests. Canvassing efforts were focused on identifying potential Brindisi voters, securing pledges of support, and ensuring turnout. Groups operated secret Facebook pages that disseminated campaign and organizing information. This was intended to protect members from potential backlash for their critical views of Donald Trump and Republicans more generally, as neighbors, bosses, and landlords, included Trump supporters. Largely comprised of women, and various minority groups, members were also acutely aware of how existing power structures could prompt animosity and discrimination. Secrecy provided strategic advantages as well, enabling the selective public dissemination of information and viewpoints, while building a level of trust and comfort as many engaged public politics for the first time.

Several grassroots organizers engaged in print and broadcast media too. The *Observer Dispatch* regularly received letters-to-the-editor criticizing Tenney, far outnumbering letters by Tenney's supporters. Organizers were also occasional guests on local radio, such as *Talk of the Town* on WUTQ in Utica, and interviewed by statewide and national media organizations, such as *Politico New York* and *The New York Times*. Grassroots organizations were responsible for weekly protests outside of Tenney's office and a large anti-Trump protest in downtown Utica when the president fundraised for Tenney. Members met with Tenney individually, and expressed concerns collectively, as possible. Organizers regularly directed members to be pointed, but not disruptive, nor break any laws. For instance, when organizers were able to attend public events with questions, they used green-and-red squares to communicate their support or opposition to Tenney's perspectives.

As a whole, grassroots organizations and efforts provided a tactical advantage for Brindisi as a form of quasi-campaign infrastructure that cost nothing, yet provided countless hours of valuable traditional and nontraditional campaign support, bolstering existing campaign and party committee structures. In contrast, Tenney often divided Republicans throughout her political rise. This was reflected in local Republican Party committees, which had pro-Tenney and Trump factions, as well as moderate Republican factions, who were more supportive of Republicans, like Richard Hanna, Joseph Griffo, and Anthony Picente. Moreover, Republican activists tended to be older and less involved than Democrats, who could better connect older and younger activists, as local college and university students tended to be more liberal than conservative. While Tenney had a small group of very passionate and dedicated supporters, their size, scope, and organization did not come close to rivaling grassroots organizing on the left.

New York State politics provided a cautionary tale for what could happen for moderate Democrats who did not sufficiently connect with progressives, even ones who had been in office for years. In September of 2018, for instance, incumbent Central New York State Senator David Valesky (District 53) was upset in the 2018 primary by Rachel May, a progressive organizer and academic professional at Syracuse University. Valesky was not as well liked by progressives as Brindisi and on occasion ridiculed grassroots members for raising the prospect of a primary challenge to him. When May declared, Valesky appeared confident in retaining his seat, and did not actively campaign. This was probably part of strategic effort to avoid antagonizing progressive Democrats in the district, yet harmed his general election changes. May did not have to fend off public criticism and generated optimal turnout in more liberal portions of the district. The lesson learned for Democratic incumbents was to fully ingratiate themselves with progressives because no other group was as enthusiastic and willing to volunteer their time for political mobilization. Brindisi recognized this well in advance and seamlessly incorporated progressive groups into his election efforts from the outset.

One related and unique dimension of New York elections is how candidates can run on multiple ballot lines in New York State. In other words, candidates are often listed as nominees of multiple parties. For example, a conservative candidate is typically the nominee of the Republican Party and the Conservative Party. Securing the Independence Party endorsement was an early focus of the Brindisi campaign. The party also endorsed Katko and Faso. Independence Party vote shares for Katko and Brindisi exceeded 2 percent respectively. This may not seem like much, given the two major party lines comprise the vast majority vote shares for candidates, but it is sizeable enough to make a difference in close elections. Brindisi's ability to secure the Independence Party endorsement, the only Democrat in the races examined here to do so, helped to further his independent and bipartisan credentials, while appealing to moderately conservative voters.

In NY-24, Dana Balter came to electoral politics through grassroots organizing as a member of the CNY Solidarity Coalition from its inception, shortly after the election of Donald Trump. The coalition described itself as "a grassroots coalition of organizations and individuals committed to protecting all Central New Yorkers from the dangers of the Trump-Pence-Ryan administration's policies, appointees, and rhetoric."[112] The coalition was "dedicated to truth, justice, and democracy" and aimed "to protect and fight alongside People of Color, Immigrants, Refugees, LGBTQI people, the Muslim Community, the Jewish Community, Women, People with Disabilities, People with Mental Illness, the Deaf Community, Teachers, Scientists, Environmentalists, and all other marginalized and oppressed groups and entities that are likely to be targeted in these uncertain times." As the name implies, the coalition involved existing organizations, such as the Syracuse Peace Council, Workers' Center of Central New York, the Central New York Area Labor Federation, Syracuse Cultural Workers, and Urban Jobs Task Force, while drawing upon new members, who became more politically active in response to the Trump presidency.

The organization operated more as an autonomous entity than a coalition. Similar to what Skocpol found in other parts of the country, college-educated suburban women had a significant role. Some of these women were politically active prior to the Trump presidency. Some were not. While there were people of color present at the beginning, not all felt welcome, making racial diversity a challenge. In response, CNY Solidarity brought in outside training to help with this. In contrast to Skocpol's findings, men have been relatively equally involved in leadership, and the coalition is more progressive than moderate in terms of political beliefs. In NY-22, grassroots leaders and volunteers were predominately women.

Local media described CNY Solidarity Coalition as "one of the most visible groups of local protesters to spring up" since the 2016 election. The coalition "became an overnight political force, attracting the attention of Democratic leaders like Mayor Stephanie Miner and antagonizing Congressional Republicans like John Katko" as a "unified, motivated and angry group of people who are gearing up for a long-term fight."[113] The coalition did not endorse candidates, but as members started running for office, including Rachel May and Dana Balter, Indivisible NY-24 was formed by a group of CNY Solidarity Coalition members focused on policy and policymakers. Indivisible NY-24 endorsed and supported Balter in the NY-24 Democratic primary. In the general election, the group launched a sustained public opposition campaign against John Katko. Indivisible NY-24 developed petitions, organized protests, including regular ones outside of Katko's office focused on various issues, and coordinated mass phone call efforts to Katko's office through weekly action alerts to members. Katko recognized the right of protesters to assemble and protest, and expressed appreciation for their passion:

> I have spoken with numerous CNY 'Indivisible' members, and invited them to meet regularly with my office to ensure their concerns are heard. Having spoken with several of these individuals, I have seen that many of them are sincere, and truly want to engage in a constructive conversation. I have and will continue to make myself available to such individuals.[114]

Indivisible NY-24 was particularly critical of Katko for not holding town halls open to the public. In 2014, Katko criticized his first opponent Dan Maffei for "his weak record regarding open meetings."[115] Indivisible NY-24 organizer Thomas Keck described a regular pattern surrounding protests at Katko's office where they would ask to meet with Katko; then after being denied, ask if he was there; then after not getting an answer, ask if they would send staff down to visit with them; and then after being denied, ask if they could send members up to meet with staff. On occasion, Katko's staff would visit with small groups of protesters without cameras. Keck, who is also the Michael O. Sawyer Chair of Constitutional Law and Politics at Syracuse University's Maxwell School, thought Katko avoided unscripted environments because these did not play to his political strengths. Keck also believed this was part of a larger strategy adopted by the Republican Party to avoid town halls after related video clips negatively portraying GOP incumbents went viral.

Katko was critical of grassroots organizers at times, contending this "small but vocal" group of protesters were after "theatrics," whereas his telephone town halls and listening sessions provided efficient and substantive dialogue.[116] "This is a movement nationwide," Katko explained, "where the whole design is to get you in front of a camera in front of 700, 800 people and not let you talk."[117] Indivisible "claims to be interested in productive, public discourse with their federal representatives," but its "playbook instructs just the opposite" by advising members to bombard Congressmen with phone calls and encouraging disruptive behavior at town hall meetings, including interrupting, booing, and chanting.[118] Katko lamented how "opportunities for constructive engagement between citizens and their representatives" were turned "into unruly spectacles where constructive engagement is impossible" and asserted:

> These individuals are preventing members of my staff from helping refugees, senior citizens, and veterans. By flooding my office with hundreds of calls and holding regular protests, they are only hurting their neighbors—veterans in need of VA Hospital care, seniors dependent on Social Security and Medicare, individuals facing pressing immigration matters, and local organizations seeking to apply for federal grants.[119]

The two sides connected on rare occasions. In March of 2017, for instance, Katko spoke with a group of protesters from CNY Solidarity, including Dana Balter, who had gathered outside of a fundraising event. Katko answered questions about various issues, and the Trump administration, pledging to vote with Democrats if legislation was proposed to have the president share his tax history. Katko also fielded criticism about his public availability for town halls, citing his willingness to visit with the constituents who had gathered, and highlighting the rigorous schedule of being a federal representative. When someone suggested that he was afraid to hold a town hall, Katko referenced death threats he and his family received as a federal prosecutor. "You can call me a lot of things," Katko retorted, "but I'm not afraid of anything."[120]

Indivisible NY-24 and Indivisible Mohawk Valley shared many parallels in terms of organization, goals, messaging, and approach. There were some notable differences too. Indivisible Mohawk Valley devoted greater focus and energy to canvassing during the general election campaign. Indivisible NY-24 was active in helping Balter secure the

Democratic nomination in a contested primary, no small feat, but receded some afterwards. Democrats were unified in NY-22, enabling grassroots organizers to devote all their attention to defeating the incumbent. Indivisible NY-24 heavily focused on protests and phone calls, which were successful in eroding the perception of Katko as a well-respected moderate who would remain in office for a sustained period of time, like former Congressman Jim Walsh. Unlike their counterparts in NY-24, Indivisible Mohawk Valley, and Knit the District, more generally, did not emerge from a more ideologically liberal organizing background that engaged in tactics of direct action and civil disobedience. Rather, their leaders spoke more as mothers and grandmothers, appealing to family concerns and basic democratic norms.

Like Katko, Tenney was critical of grassroots organizers. Tenney used more ideological terms in portraying the resistance as radical liberals and obstructionists to Republican control of government and the Trump presidency. This included suggesting they would shout her down if she held a true town hall-style meeting, and expressing concern about some of their signage, which Tenney found to be crude and inappropriate. At the same time, she claimed to meet with resistance members as part of her constituent outreach. There were seldom moments of agreement or mutual affection. Tenney's critics were passionately dedicated to unseating her, while Tenney claimed hate for the president so clouded the judgment of the political left that they had "bizarre Trump derangement syndrome," and sought to "vilify the president" in a manner that was "intentional" and "sinister."[121]

Grassroots organizing in NY-19 was furthered by PACs, such as NY-19 Votes, formed after the 2016 election as they put it, "new and experienced activists from all over the district were determined to resist the Trump agenda and send Congressman John Faso packing." This mission was pursued "by teaching activist how to canvass and effectively outreach to voters."[122] The belief was that defeating Faso would require transforming enthusiasm on the left into practical knowledge and skills regarding electoral politics. Healthcare was a major issue organizers discussed. Voter registration was a major procedural focus.

One unique component was targeting tens of thousands of people who owned one of multiple homes in NY-19, but were registered to vote in New York City. There was a concentrated effort to persuade these people to reregister upstate and make that process as easy as possible. Another unique component was how grassroots organizers from outside of the district, even outside the state from Connecticut and Massachusetts, volunteered to help in NY-19 because this was the nearest swing district. This could become a growing trend with significant advancements in digital communication, coupled with increased political homogenization, as people increasingly live and work in communities that reflect their political beliefs.

Organizing into a PAC helped NY-19 Votes fundraise. Lower-turnout Democratic voters and unaffiliated voters were a major focus of electoral mobilization. Dustin Reidy, founder of NY-19 Votes, believed the group's success was contingent on its collaborative nature where credit was not important. Electoral mobilization trainings sought to make efforts feel impactful, without being too burdensome or complicated. An emphasis was placed on interpersonal communication, out of the belief that this approach cuts through everything, particularly in the face of politically reinforcing social media bubbles people increasingly find themselves in.

John Faso downplayed the impact of grassroots organizers. When asked post-election about protesters who gathered outside of his district offices for "Faso Fridays," Faso believed this "didn't have a tremendous impact." Faso did acknowledge that being a Republican, and perceived as an extension of Trump, was not helpful, and that protests "made it difficult sometimes to conduct business in our office." For example, nine protesters were arrested for a sit-in at Faso's office after her did not support the DREAM Act.[123] "People were vociferous and, by and large, respectful," Faso explained. He recognized that in "a divided district a lot of people aren't going to agree with me on some issues" and defended their right to voice this disagreement.

The lesson of 2018 grassroots organizing in Central New York was that the more electorally focused these efforts were, the better positioned they were to defeat Republican incumbents. Grassroots protests clearly posed a new and fluid set of challenges for John Katko, Claudia Tenney, and John Faso. Events generated earned media that portrayed incumbent Republicans and President Trump in an unfavorable light, which put them on the defensive. At the same time, completely ignoring constituents was unfeasible. There were no great options for to how effectively manage these public displays of criticism. This left GOP incumbents in an uncomfortable middle ground between legitimizing protesters, by directly addressing their concerns, or explicitly discrediting them as disruptive or devious.

Conclusion

Central New York was a pivotal piece of the 2018 midterm election. Local races illustrated key developments and dynamics with widespread analytic utility, while also exhibiting state-specific political drama. Candidates and grassroots organizing mattered. President Trump hurt House GOP incumbents more than helped them. Republicans were forced to defend their views toward the Affordable Care Act rather than use them as political fodder. Moderate Democratic candidates were more successful than progressive ones. And New Yorkers from Donald Trump to Chuck Schumer to Andrew Cuomo were major figures on the national political landscape.

Democrats successfully regained the House, in part, by winning two of three vulnerable seats upstate in NY-19 and NY-22. Antonio Delgado and Anthony Brindisi became relatively young newcomers to Congress with proven electoral abilities. Their victories constituted the first-time Democrats won these districts since the boundaries were redrawn following the 2010 election. This could be viewed as a blessing and a curse. Replicating the successful 2018 campaigns will likely be difficult, particularly in Republican-dominated districts, such as NY-22. In NY-24, John Katko demonstrated his ability to sustain electoral success through multiple presidencies and election cycles, though Dana Balter shrunk Katko's coalition and is well positioned to improve upon her first Congressional campaign.

Through it all, Donald Trump remained the most powerful and unpredictable figure in American politics. The new 116th Congress was greeted with a government shutdown and controversial national emergency declaration by President Trump. The final two years of Trump's term, including the end of the Mueller investigation, growing legal scrutiny of the president, and a robust 2020 campaign, are poised to again reshape the electoral landscape.

Notes

1. "2014 midterm election turnout lowest in 70 years," *PBS News Hour*, November 10, 2014, https://www.pbs.org/newshour/politics/2014-midterm-election-turnout-lowest-in-70-years
2. Jay Newton-Small, "Vulnerable Democrats ran away from Obama," October 14, 2014, http://time.com/3507165/alison-grimes-barack-obama-midterm-elections/
3. David Farenthold, "GOP dominates midterms, take control of Senate," *The Washington Post*, November 5, 2014, https://www.washingtonpost.com/national/2014/11/05/4156eaf0-5330-11e4-892e-602188e70e9c_story.html?utm_term=.a722c9e22bad
4. Jason Horowitz, "Rep. Michael Grimm pleads guilty, but says he won't resign," *The New York Times*, December 23, 2014, https://www.nytimes.com/2014/12/24/nyregion/rep-michael-grimm-pleads-guilty-to-tax-fraud.html?_r=0
5. "How unpopular is Donald Trump?" *Five Thirty Eight*, November 6, 2018, https://projects.fivethirtyeight.com/trump-approval-ratings/
6. Camila Domonoske, "A Boatload of Ballots; Midterm Voter Turnout Hit 50 year High," *NPR*, November 8, 2018, https://www.npr.org/2018/11/08/665197690/a-boatload-of-ballots-midterm-voter-turnout-hit-50-year-high
7. Zach Williams and Rebecca Lewis, "New York House general election results," *City and State NY*, November 6, 2018, https://cityandstateny.com/articles/politics/campaigns-elections/new-york-congress-general-election-results-2018.html
8. Jason Horowitz, "Rep. Michael Grimm pleads guilty, but says he won't resign," *The New York Times*, December 23, 2014, https://www.nytimes.com/2014/12/24/nyregion/rep-michael-grimm-pleads-guilty-to-tax-fraud.html?_r=0
9. Alexander Burns, "Donavan, Staten Island Prosecutor, Wins Congressional seat Grimm held," *The New York Times*, May 5, 2015, https://www.nytimes.com/2015/05/06/nyregion/daniel-donovan-elected-to-congress-from-new-york.html
10. Lisa Foderaro, "Democrats Hope to Beat New York City's Only G.O.P. Congressman, It Won't Be Easy," *The New York Times*, September 27, 2018, https://www.nytimes.com/2018/09/27/nyregion/dan-donovan-staten-island-trump-max-rose.html
11. Lisa Foderaro, "Democrats Hope to Beat New York City's Only G.O.P. Congressman, It Won't Be Easy," *The New York Times*, September 27, 2018, https://www.nytimes.com/2018/09/27/nyregion/dan-donovan-staten-island-trump-max-rose.html

12. Lisa Foderaro, "Democrats Hope to Beat New York City's Only G.O.P. Congressman, It Won't Be Easy," *The New York Times*, September 27, 2018, https://www.nytimes.com/2018/09/27/nyregion/dan-donovan-staten-island-trump-max-rose.html
13. Zach Williams and Rebecca Lewis, "New York House general election results," *City and State NY*, November 6, 2018, https://cityandstateny.com/articles/politics/campaigns-elections/new-york-congress-general-election-results-2018.html
14. Chris Baker, "It's over. Anthony Brindisi defeats Tenney in 22nd Congressional Race," Syracuse.com, November 20, 2018, https://www.syracuse.com/politics/index.ssf/2018/11/its_over_brindisi_defeats_tenney_in_22nd_congressional_race.html
15. Dispatch Staff, "After 3 week, NY-22 race is settled," *Oneida Daily Dispatch*, November 28, 2018, https://www.oneidadispatch.com/news/after-three-weeks-ny%2D%2Drace-is-settled/article_8fbbb202-f354-11e8-b068-b7b7cc869674.html
16. Natasha Vaughn, "Five things to know about Anthony Brindisi's post-election plans," *Binghamton Press & Sun Bulletin*, December 6, 2018, https://www.pressconnects.com/story/news/local/2018/12/06/anthony-brindisi-congress-agenda-ny-22-district/2192369002/
17. Michael Lewis-Beck and Charles Tien, "Congressional Election Forecasting: Structure-X Models for 2014," *PS: Political Science and Politics*, 47.4 (October 2014): 782.
18. Michael Lewis-Beck and Charles Tien, "Congressional Election Forecasting: Structure-X Models for 2014," *PS: Political Science and Politics*, 47.4 (October 2014): 782.
19. Joseph Bafumi, Robert Erikson, Christopher Wlezien, "Balancing, Generic Polls and Midterm Congressional Elections," *The Journal of Politics*, 72.3 (July 2010): 705–706.
20. Jeffrey Jones, "Midterm Seat Loss Averages 37 for Unpopular Presidents," *Gallup*, September 12, 2018. https://news.gallup.com/poll/242093/midterm-seat-loss-averages-unpopular-presidents.aspx
21. Joseph Bafumi, Robert Erikson, Christopher Wlezien, "Balancing, Generic Polls and Midterm Congressional Elections," *The Journal of Politics*, 72.3 (July 2010): 706.
22. Rachel Bitecofer, "Signs, Signs, Everywhere Are Signs: Why Democrats Will Win Big in the 2018 Midterms," Wason Center Blog, September 26, 2018, http://wasoncenter.cnu.edu/signs-signs-everywhere-are-signs-why-democrats-will-win-big-in-the-2018-midterms/

23. "How Popular is Donald Trump?" *Five Thirty Eight*, November 8, 2018, https://projects.fivethirtyeight.com/trump-approval-ratings/?ex_cid=irpromo
24. Matthew Ylegias. "Donald Trump, the resistance, the limits of normcore politics." *Vox.* July 3, 2018. https://www.vox.com/2018/7/3/17379766/trump-norms-democracy
25. Will Kane. "White house resistance to Trump unlike anything before; Berkley politics expert argues." *Berkley News.* September 6, 2018. http://news.berkeley.edu/2018/09/06/white-house-resistance-to-trump-is-unlike-anything-before-berkeley-politics-expert-argues/
26. Phillip Bump, "Trump has embraced campaign rallies," *The Washington Post,* October 10, 2018, https://www.washingtonpost.com/politics/2018/10/10/trump-has-embraced-campaign-rallies-golf-remains-his-true-love/?utm_term=.9ae44240257f
27. David Jackson, "Trump hones campaign themes: Kavanaugh, impeachment, nicknames," *USA Today,* October 22, 2018, https://www.usatoday.com/story/news/politics/elections/2018/10/17/donald-trump-midterm-themes-kavanaugh-impeachment-nicknames/1590500002/
28. Chris Cadelago, "Trump's midterm pitch: vote for me," *Politico*, October 10, 2018, https://www.politico.com/story/2018/10/10/trump-midterm-pitch-886196
29. Amina Dunn, John Laloggia, and Carroll Doherty, "In midterm voting decisions, policy took back seat to partisanship," *Pew Research Center*, November 29, 2018, http://www.pewresearch.org/fact-tank/2018/11/29/in-midterm-voting-decisions-policies-took-a-back-seat-to-partisanship/
30. Luke Perry, "*NY-22 Minute: Tenney on Trump – 'Most Successful Presidency in Modern History,'*" Utica College Center of Public Affairs and Election Research, May 23, 2018, https://www.ucpublicaffairs.com/home/2018/5/23/2ug497y7z5cbqvc6sg1eix3mnmzzi0
31. Video available at: https://talkingpointsmemo.com/livewire/claudia-tenney-fake-news-remark-mass-murderers-democrats
32. Allison Graves, "Viral Image about Florida Baseless," *Politifact*, August 9, 2016, https://www.politifact.com/florida/statements/2016/aug/09/viral-image/viral-image-about-voter-fraud-completely-baseless/
33. Cassie Owens, "Internet: Philly Rigged the 2012 Election. Experts: Still No," *Politifact*, August 12, 2016, https://www.politifact.com/pennsylvania/statements/2016/aug/12/viral-image/internet-philly-rigged-2012-presidential-election-/

34. Nadia Pflaum, "Viral post alleges voter fraud in Wood County, OH," *Politifact*, August 16, 2016, https://www.politifact.com/ohio/statements/2016/aug/16/viral-image/viral-post-alleges-voter-fraud-wood-county-ohio/
35. C. Eugene Emery, "Viral post claiming voter fraud in 2012 election errs on photo id numbers," *Politifact*, August 9, 2016, https://www.politifact.com/truth-o-meter/statements/2016/aug/09/viral-image/viral-post-claiming-voter-fraud-2012-election-errs/.
36. Linda Qui, "Trump's baseless claims about the election being 'rigged,'" *Politifact*, August 15, 2016, https://www.politifact.com/truth-o-meter/statements/2016/aug/15/donald-trump/donald-trumps-baseless-claims-about-election-being/
37. Amy Sherman, "Following Trump voter fraud allegations, claim that 5.7 million noncitizens voted in wrong," *Politifact*, June 22, 2017, https://www.politifact.com/florida/statements/2017/jun/22/ainsley-earhardt/following-trump-voter-fraud-allegations-claim-57-m/
38. Luke Perry, "NY-22 Minute: Tenney Believes 'Deep State' Responsible for Ben Carson's Office Furniture," Utica College Center of Public Affairs and Election Research, March 21, 2018, https://www.ucpublicaffairs.com/home/2018/3/21/ny-22-minute-tenney-believes-deep-state-responsible-for-ben-carsons-office-furniture-by-luke-perry
39. Jon Greenberg, "Trump says collusion is not a crime. That's not right." *Politifact*, July 31, 2018, https://www.politifact.com/truth-o-meter/statements/2018/jul/31/donald-trump/donald-trump-says-collusion-no-crime-right/
40. "Ex-Trump Attorney Michael Cohen Pleads Guilty to Campaign Finance Violations," *CBS News*, August 21, 2018, https://www.cbsnews.com/news/michael-cohen-plea-deal-details-today-2018-08-21/
41. Luke Perry, "NY-22 Minute: Tenney Joins 10 Republicans Calling for Investigation of Comey, Clinton, & More," Utica College Center of Public Affairs and Election Research, April 18, 2018, https://www.ucpublicaffairs.com/home/2018/4/18/ny-22-minute-tenney-joins-10-republicans-calling-for-investigation-of-comey-clinton-more-by-luke-perry
42. Andrew Donavan, "President Trump Tweets: 'Vote Claudia!' in New York's 22nd District," *Local SYR.com*, November 5, 2018, https://www.localsyr.com/news/local-news/president-trump-tweets-vote-claudia-in-new-york-s-22nd-district/1574009179
43. Luke Perry, "Comparing John Katko (NY-24) and Claudia Tenney (NY-22): Trump Endorsement," Utica College Center of Public Affairs and Election Research, August 27, 2018, https://www.ucpublicaffairs.com/home/2018/8/27/john-katko-

44. Mark Weiner, "Rep. John Katko on Mueller Investigation: 'It's not a witch hunt," Syracuse.com, August 22, 2018, https://www.syracuse.com/politics/index.ssf/2018/08/rep_john_katko_on_mueller_investigation_its_not_a_witch_hunt.html
45. This data was retrieved from Tracking Congress in the Age of Trump by *Five Thirty Eight* available at https://projects.fivethirtyeight.com/congress-trump-score/house/
46. Mark Weiner, "Rep. John Katko: Trump follower or independent voice? A look at 11 key votes," Syracuse.com, July 31, 2018, https://www.syracuse.com/expo/news/erry-2018/07/aed9a4ab9f1853/rep-john-katko-trump-follower.html
47. Luke Perry, "Comparing John Katko (NY-24) and Claudia Tenney (NY-22): Trump Endorsement," Utica College Center of Public Affairs and Election Research, August 27, 2018, https://www.ucpublicaffairs.com/home/2018/8/27/john-katko-
48. Luke Perry, "John Katko Talks Congress, Campaign, Sessions, and Trump," Utica College Center of Public Affairs and Election Research, September 12, 2018, https://www.ucpublicaffairs.com/home/2018/9/10/john-katko-ny-24-talks-congress-campaign-sessions-trump-with-luke-perry
49. William Kemple, "Rep. Faso 'Disappointed' by Trump's response to Russia interference in US matters," *Daily Freemen*, March 26, 2018, https://www.dailyfreeman.com/news/rep-faso-disappointed-by-trump-s-response-to-russian-interference/article_6a28f44e-4d98-5dc5-9cc5-fd42b24a898a.html
50. "Faso criticizes Trump's unwillingness to blame Putin for election meddling" *Hudson Valley One*, July 16, 2018, https://hudsonvalleyone.com/2018/07/16/faso-criticizes-trumps-unwillingness-to-blame-putin-for-election-meddling/
51. Nina Schutzman, "John Faso endorsed by President Trump in 19th District Race," *Poughkeepsie Journal*, October 23, 2018, https://www.poughkeepsiejournal.com/story/news/local/2018/10/23/john-faso-endorsed-president-trump-19th-district-race/1739680002/
52. Jeff Mason and Roberta Rampton, "Defiant Trump blames media, fellow Republicans for House lost," *Reuters*, November 7, 2018, https://www.reuters.com/article/us-usa-election-trump-press/defiant-trump-blames-media-fellow-republicans-for-house-losses-idUSKCN1NC2ND
53. John Faso made these comments in an interview conducted by *Bloomberg* available at https://www.bloomberg.com/news/videos/2018-11-13/rep-faso-says-he-wouldn-t-have-won-by-embracing-trump-video
54. John Faso made these comments in an interview conducted by *Bloomberg* available at https://www.bloomberg.com/news/videos/2018-11-13/rep-faso-says-he-wouldn-t-have-won-by-embracing-trump-video

55. Amanda Purcell, "Faso reflects on what might have been," *Hudson Valley 360*, December 6, 2018, https://www.hudsonvalley360.com/article/faso-reflects-what-might-have-been
56. Amanda Purcell, "Faso reflects on what might have been," *Hudson Valley 360*, December 6, 2018, https://www.hudsonvalley360.com/article/faso-reflects-what-might-have-been
57. Dan Freedman, "Tale of two NY Republicans: a winner and loser," *Times Union*, November 29, 2018. https://www.timesunion.com/7day-state/article/Tale-of-two-N-Y-Republicans-A-winner-and-a-loser-13432643.php
58. Patrick Lynch, "Midterm Elections and Economic Fluctuations: The Response of Voters Over Time," *Legislative Studies Quarterly*, 27.2 (May 2002): 269–270.
59. Michael Lewis-Beck and Charles Tien, "Congressional Election Forecasting: Structure-X Models for 2014," *PS: Political Science and Politics*, 47.4 (October 2014): 782.
60. U.S. Bureau of Economic Analysis, "U.S. Economy at a Glance," Accessed December 15, 2018, https://www.bea.gov/news/glance
61. Erik Wasson and Sho Chandra, "'Trump Effect' Overpowers Booming Economy Ahead of Midterms," *Bloomberg*, October 19, 2018, https://www.bloomberg.com/news/articles/2018-10-19/-trump-effect-overpowers-booming-economy-as-driver-in-midterms
62. Paul Davidson and Adam Shell, "Trade wars, taxes, and immigration, among top economic issues for voters in 2018," *USA Today*, November 5, 2018, https://www.usatoday.com/story/money/2018/11/05/midterm-elections-economy/1856916002/
63. Paul Davidson and Adam Shell, "Trade wars, taxes, and immigration, among top economic issues for voters in 2018," *USA Today*, November 5, 2018, https://www.usatoday.com/story/money/2018/11/05/midterm-elections-economy/1856916002/
64. Josh Boak, "Why aren't many Americans benefitting from a robust economy?" *USA Today*, June 15, 2018, https://www.usatoday.com/story/money/economy/2018/06/15/why-many-americans-arent-benefiting-robust-us-economy/705655002/
65. Josh Boak, "Why aren't many Americans benefitting from a robust economy?" *USA Today*, June 15, 2018, https://www.usatoday.com/story/money/economy/2018/06/15/why-many-americans-arent-benefiting-robust-us-economy/705655002/
66. "President Trump Job Approval- The Economy," *Real Clear Politics*, accessed December 15, 2018, https://www.realclearpolitics.com/epolls/other/president_trump_job_approval_economy-6182.html#polls

67. Aimee Picchi, "Is Trump Right that it's the best economy and jobs EVER?" *CBS News,* June 5, 2018, https://www.cbsnews.com/news/trump-economy-jobs-best-ever-tweet-today-fact-check-2018-06-04/
68. Erik Wasson and Sho Chandra, "'Trump Effect' Overpowers Booming Economy Ahead of Midterms," *Bloomberg,* October 19, 2018, https://www.bloomberg.com/news/articles/2018-10-19/-trump-effect-overpowers-booming-economy-as-driver-in-midterms
69. Byron York, "Of course Trump is talking about the economy. Who says he's not?" *Washington Examiner,* November 5, 2018, https://www.washingtonexaminer.com/opinion/of-course-trump-is-talking-about-the-economy-who-says-hes-not
70. Robert Harding, "Five reasons why Rep. John Katko won reelection in House race against Dana Balter," *The Citizen,* November 8, 2018, https://auburnpub.com/blogs/eye_on_ny/five-reasons-why-rep-john-katko-won-re-election-in/article_b81ae282-e25a-11e8-bcbe-ab3d15ea16b2.html
71. Robert Harding, "Five reasons why Rep. John Katko won reelection in House race against Dana Balter," *The Citizen,* November 8, 2018, https://auburnpub.com/blogs/eye_on_ny/five-reasons-why-rep-john-katko-won-re-election-in/article_b81ae282-e25a-11e8-bcbe-ab3d15ea16b2.html
72. Lisa Foderaro, *National Democrats Wade, Uninvited, Into New York House Race, The New York Times,* May 30, 2018, https://www.nytimes.com/2018/05/30/nyregion/perez-williams-katko-balter-syracuse-house-election.html
73. Lisa Foderaro, *National Democrats Wade, Uninvited, Into New York House Race, The New York Times,* May 30, 2018, https://www.nytimes.com/2018/05/30/nyregion/perez-williams-katko-balter-syracuse-house-election.html
74. Mark Weiner, "Why were NY-24 polls so off?" Syracuse.com, June 28, 2018, https://www.syracuse.com/politics/index.ssf/2018/06/why_was_ny-24_poll_so_off_dana_balter_finished_strong_pollster_says.html
75. Robert Harding, "Dana Balter takes money lead over GOP Rep. Katko in final weeks of election," *Auburnpub.com,* October 26, 2018, https://auburnpub.com/blogs/eye_on_ny/democrat-balter-takes-money-lead-over-gop-rep-katko-in/article_afdff7ac-d89f-11e8-bbba-13df4f9aa562.html
76. Robert Harding, "Eye on NY: Dana Balter reflects on 'phenomenal' campaign for Congress," *Auburnpub.com,* November 26, 2018, https://www.syracuse.com/politics/index.ssf/2018/06/why_was_ny-24_poll_so_off_dana_balter_finished_strong_pollster_says.html

77. Bridget Bowman, "Meet the Challengers Who Outraised House Incumbents," *Roll Call,* October 18, 2017, https://www.rollcall.com/news/politics/meet-challengers-outraised-house-incumbents
78. Andrew Solender, "Out-of-district donations dominate congressional fundraising," *City and State NY,* September 18, 2018, https://www.cityandstateny.com/articles/politics/campaigns-elections/new-york-congressional-fundraising-out-of-district-donations.html
79. Samantha Madison, "No reimbursement coming for Trump's Utica visit," *Observer Dispatch,* September 12, 2018, https://www.uticaod.com/news/20180912/no-reimbursement-coming-for-trumps-utica-visit
80. Luke Perry, "NY-22 Minute: Tenney States Many Murderers Are Democrats," Utica College Center of Public Affairs and Election Research, February 21, 2018, https://www.ucpublicaffairs.com/home/2018/2/21/ny-22-minute-tenney-states-many-mass-murderers-are-democrats-by-luke-perry
81. Luke Perry, "NY-22 Minute: Tenney States Many Murderers Are Democrats," Utica College Center of Public Affairs and Election Research, February 21, 2018, https://www.ucpublicaffairs.com/home/2018/2/21/ny-22-minute-tenney-states-many-mass-murderers-are-democrats-by-luke-perry
82. Luke Perry, "Sockpuppet Social," *Stateline NY,* October 5, 2018, https://statelineny.atavist.com/sockpuppet-social?preview
83. Andrew Solender, "John Faso has one problem, and it's Antonio Delgado," *Chronogram,* November 1, 2018, https://www.chronogram.com/hudsonvalley/john-faso-has-one-problem-and-its-antonio-delgado/Content?oid=6671617
84. Andrew Solender, "John Faso has one problem, and it's Antonio Delgado," *Chronogram,* November 1, 2018, https://www.chronogram.com/hudsonvalley/john-faso-has-one-problem-and-its-antonio-delgado/Content?oid=6671617
85. Andrew Solender, "John Faso has one problem, and it's Antonio Delgado," *Chronogram,* November 1, 2018, https://www.chronogram.com/hudsonvalley/john-faso-has-one-problem-and-its-antonio-delgado/Content?oid=6671617
86. Chris McKenna, "Delgado Leads NY-19 Democrats in Fundraising," *Times Herald Record,* January 13, 2018, https://www.recordonline.com/news/20180113/fray-delgado-leads-ny19-democrats-in-4th-quarter-fundraising
87. Jesse Smith, "In congressional race, Delgado rakes in more than Faso, but campaigns very close in cash-on-hand," *Hudson Valley One,* October 19, 2018, https://hudsonvalleyone.com/2018/10/19/in-congressional-race-delgado-rakes-in-more-than-faso-but-campaigns-very-close-in-cash-on-hand/

88. Andrew Solender, "Out-of-district donations dominate congressional fundraising," *City and State NY*, September 18, 2018, https://www.cityandstateny.com/articles/politics/campaigns-elections/new-york-congressional-fundraising-out-of-district-donations.html
89. Erica Chenowith and Jeremy Pressman. "This is what we learned by counting the women's marches." *The Monkey Cage*. February 7, 2017. https://www.washingtonpost.com/news/monkey-cage/wp/2017/02/07/this-is-what-we-learned-by-counting-the-womens-marches/?utm_term=.4d50d478d7e8
90. This was retrieved from Indivisible's website at https://indivisible.org/about
91. This was retrieved from Indivisible's website at https://indivisible.org/about
92. Lara Putnam and Theda Skocpol, "Middle America Reboots Democracy," *Democracy*, February 20, 2018, https://democracyjournal.org/arguments/middle-america-reboots-democracy/
93. Gideon Lewis-Kraus, "How the 'Resistance' Helped Democrats Dominate Virginia," *The New York Times*, November 13, 2017, https://www.nytimes.com/2017/11/13/magazine/how-the-resistance-helped-democrats-dominate-virginia.html
94. Heather Yates, "Body slamming in the Big Sky State," *The Utica College Center of Public Affairs and Election Research*, May 26, 2017, https://www.ucpublicaffairs.com/home/2017/5/26/body-slamming-in-the-big-sky-state-by-heather-e-yates
95. Heather Yates, "Doug Jones Turns Alabama Blue in Special Election," *The Utica College Center of Public Affairs and Election Research*, December 13, 2017, https://www.ucpublicaffairs.com/home/2017/12/13/doug-jones-turns-alabama-blue-in-special-election-by-heather-e-yates
96. Van Newkirk, "How Grassroots Organizers Got Black Voters to the Polls in Alabama," *The Atlantic*, December 17, 2017, https://www.theatlantic.com/politics/archive/2017/12/sparking-an-electoral-revival-in-alabama/548504/
97. Van Newkirk, "How Grassroots Organizers Got Black Voters to the Polls in Alabama," *The Atlantic*, December 17, 2017, https://www.theatlantic.com/politics/archive/2017/12/sparking-an-electoral-revival-in-alabama/548504/
98. Van Newkirk, "How Grassroots Organizers Got Black Voters to the Polls in Alabama," *The Atlantic*, December 17, 2017, https://www.theatlantic.com/politics/archive/2017/12/sparking-an-electoral-revival-in-alabama/548504/

99. Van Newkirk, "How Grassroots Organizers Got Black Voters to the Polls in Alabama," *The Atlantic*, December 17, 2017, https://www.theatlantic.com/politics/archive/2017/12/sparking-an-electoral-revival-in-alabama/548504/
100. Theda Skocpol, "Can Marches Become Movements" *Democracy*, February 2, 2017, https://democracyjournal.org/arguments/can-marches-become-a-movement/
101. Theda Skocpol, "Can Marches Become Movements" *Democracy*, February 2, 2017, https://democracyjournal.org/arguments/can-marches-become-a-movement/
102. Lara Putnam and Theda Skocpol, "Middle America Reboots Democracy," *Democracy*, February 20, 2018, https://democracyjournal.org/arguments/middle-america-reboots-democracy/
103. Lara Putnam and Theda Skocpol, "Middle America Reboots Democracy," *Democracy*, February 20, 2018, https://democracyjournal.org/arguments/middle-america-reboots-democracy/
104. Lara Putnam and Theda Skocpol, "Middle America Reboots Democracy," *Democracy*, February 20, 2018, https://democracyjournal.org/arguments/middle-america-reboots-democracy/
105. Ella Nilsen, "Progressive Democrats running in competitive House districts had a bad night on Tuesday," *Vox*, November 7, 2018, https://www.vox.com/2018/11/7/18071700/progressive-democrats-house-midterm-elections-2018
106. Ella Nilsen, "Progressive Democrats running in competitive House districts had a bad night on Tuesday," *Vox*, November 7, 2018, https://www.vox.com/2018/11/7/18071700/progressive-democrats-house-midterm-elections-2018
107. Dylan Scott, "Democrats are running to the middle to win the midterms," *Vox*, November 5, 2018, https://www.vox.com/policy-and-politics/2018/11/5/18042804/2018-midterm-elections-moderates-indiana-ohio-west-virginia
108. Dylan Scott, "Democrats are running to the middle to win the midterms," *Vox*, November 5, 2018, https://www.vox.com/policy-and-politics/2018/11/5/18042804/2018-midterm-elections-moderates-indiana-ohio-west-virginia
109. Lisa Foderaro, "To Unseat a Trump Republican, Democrats Embrace a Centrist Candidate," *The New York Times*, August 9, 2018, https://www.nytimes.com/2018/08/09/nyregion/brindisi-tenney-midterm-election-ny.html
110. Lisa Foderaro, "To Unseat a Trump Republican, Democrats Embrace a Centrist Candidate," *The New York Times*, August 9, 2018, https://www.nytimes.com/2018/08/09/nyregion/brindisi-tenney-midterm-election-ny.html

111. Lisa Foderaro, "To Unseat a Trump Republican, Democrats Embrace a Centrist Candidate," *The New York Times*, August 9, 2018, https://www.nytimes.com/2018/08/09/nyregion/brindisi-tenney-midterm-election-ny.html
112. This was retrieved from CNY Solidarity Coalition's website at https://www.cnysolidarity.org/whoweare/
113. Chris Baker, "Syracuse's leftist Tea Party: Meet the protesters behind the 1,000 person airport rally," Syracuse.com, January 31, 2017, https://www.syracuse.com/news/index.ssf/2017/01/syracuses_left-leaning_tea_party_how_trump_energized_1000s_of_protesters.html
114. "Katko Statement Concerning the Importance of Constituent Services to New York's 24th District," February 16, 2017, https://katko.house.gov/media-center/press-releases/katko-statement-concerning-importance-constituent-services-new-york-s
115. John Katko, "Enough of Dan Maffei's 'speculative ideas' for improving the economy," *Syracuse.com*, February 20, 2014, https://www.syracuse.com/opinion/index.ssf/2014/02/enough_of_rep_dan_maffeis_speculative_ideas_for_improving_the_economy_commentary.html
116. Ken Sturtz, "Demonstrators again call for Rep. Katko to hold in person town halls," Syracuse.com, February 22, 2017, https://www.syracuse.com/news/index.ssf/2017/02/demonstrators_again_call_for_rep_katko_to_hold_in-person_town_hall.html
117. Ken Sturtz, "Demonstrators again call for Rep. Katko to hold in person town halls," Syracuse.com, February 22, 2017, https://www.syracuse.com/news/index.ssf/2017/02/demonstrators_again_call_for_rep_katko_to_hold_in-person_town_hall.html
118. "Katko Statement Concerning the Importance of Constituent Services to New York's 24th District," February 16, 2017, https://katko.house.gov/media-center/press-releases/katko-statement-concerning-importance-constituent-services-new-york-s
119. "Katko Statement Concerning the Importance of Constituent Services to New York's 24th District," February 16, 2017, https://katko.house.gov/media-center/press-releases/katko-statement-concerning-importance-constituent-services-new-york-s
120. Catie O'Toole, "Rep. John Katko speaks with 75 constituents outside of Blarney Stone," Syracuse.com, March 7, 2017, https://www.syracuse.com/politics/index.ssf/2017/03/rep_john_katko_speaks_with_75_protesters_outside_blarney_stone_in_syracuse_video.html
121. Luke Perry, "NY-22 Minute: Tenney States Democrats Have Bizarre Trump Derangement Syndrome," *The Utica College Center of Public Affairs and Election Research*, February 8, 2018, https://www.ucpublicaffairs.com/home/2018/2/8/ny-22-minute-tenney-states-democrats-suffer-from-bizarre-trump-derangement-syndrome-by-luke-perry

122. "NY 19 Votes Team: Our Story" retrieved from https://www.ny19votes.com/about/
123. Amanda Purcell, "Organizers arrested at Faso protest," *Hudson Valley 360,* December 18, 2017, https://www.hudsonvalley360.com/article/organizers-arrested-faso-protest

CPSIA information can be obtained
at www.ICGtesting.com
Printed in the USA
LVHW072201250319
611824LV00016B/240/P